Book of One :-)

Volume 4

Lightworker's Log

SAM

This book is dedicated to those newly awakened parts of humanity. May you find and celebrate the Peace and Wholeness already within and know it is in serving one another that we prosper. Love is a goal that brings all things together. This focus is now permeating earth more rapidly with each energy surge.

Contents

Preface

As a reluctant wayshower, I never expected to publish another book but now am guided to do so as humanity moves rapidly toward total destruction of the old to make way for higher, more life-affirming energies. Allow the Light within to guide you and know **you are never alone!**

Earth life is a balance of giving and receiving. Maintain this balance in all you do to move through the portals to greater awareness of our True Identity, One, Perfect BEingness of Love and Light. Live in the moment of Now and follow synchronicities.

Shine on :-)

SAM
Fall 2018
Fort Lauderdale, Florida

~ **Part One** ~

Higher Realm Messages

Be aware of your propensity to relive the past. Keep the golden Light within and use it as a mirror. It will be needed in the days ahead.

Higher Realm Messages
~ A ~

All is well in your world despite your egotic attempts to convince you otherwise.

A Brand New Beginning

"You are on the cusp of awakening to a brand new beginning. This beginning is for all humanity and not limited to any one entity. We are with you now as you motor through these changes on your earth. The time of recognizing Christ Consciousness is here and we are with you to help make this transition as smooth as possible. The days before humanity now will be lighter with newer energies to carry all Home to the Oneness from whence you came. Keep within your own state of knowing and know that you are one of many helping humanity to motor through the Matrix of ease and grace.

"We are the White Winged Consciousness of Nine here to assist."

ಬ 📖 ಚ

A Field Of Receptivity Within Illusion

"Let's be clear. All is illusion. All is illusion on earth and all you can see. All is illusion on earth and all you can hear. All is illusion on earth and all you can smell. All is illusion on earth and all you sense with the five usual senses.

"But when you allow yourself the pleasure of tapping into that sixth sense, that one vital ingredient for each human, you begin to see there is more. There is more to the illusion than what one can detect from using only the five usual human senses.

"Take the time to tap into this field of receptivity to change your world, to make your human existence better. Take the time to tap into this sixth sense, to know I AM, to know you are that of which *It* is. Be still and know."

ଐ 📖 ଓ

All Are Connected:
Mass Consciousness Awakening

"You are moving quickly toward a mass consciousness awakening. We are the White Winged Consciousness of Nine and we are here to report. Those not yet ready to awaken to the truth of BEing will be consumed with the separation that is now rampant upon earth."

(As a conscious channel, I question the use of the word consumed and am told it is the best word to use.)

"This is not to say that those within that consciousness of separation will be eaten alive but yet they will be consumed, focusing all attention on separation. And as this separation continues to rule their world, it shall consume not only their thoughts but their body as well.

"When first upon your beloved earth, your bodies were not made to be as dense. They were not made to be separate in thought, in word, or deed. They were meant to be a joyous occasion, to glorify the Oneness within all, to celebrate this truth. But this is not the state of the earth today and as those knowing the truth move towards this Oneness, in essence, those not knowing the truth move away further from the Oneness.

"As your news reports this separation, and focuses totally on this separation, those living within that thought system will no longer be able to free themselves into the Oneness of which many now awaken. And yet, many other humans will awaken to this truth. They will be brought to a point where they recognize the Oneness of all Life and Truth. Many humans are now struggling to survive within your world and this is leading them to that Oneness. For as they struggle, those awakened see their struggle and seek to help. Those able to help in this knowingness of Oneness will do so and those awakening will continue to reach the fruition of their efforts through the knowledge that **all are connected**.

"All humans connected upon this earth will sense this connection. All humans upon this earth now move steadily toward either the separation of the individual from Oneness or the coalescing of the Oneness for all.

"We are the White Winged Consciousness of Nine here to report and help those ready to awaken to the truth of being one form in essence, one form in Truth, one form in Light."

ರು 📖 ೞ

Ask For Guidance

"Watching over humanity is a practice of which we have participated in for aeons of time. We are the White Winged Consciousness of Nine and we continue to watch over humanity, guiding those who wish to be guided.

"Do you wish to be guided, to your greater good, to the blessing you yourself have created, have planned for aeons of time? You see, we are you in another form. We are a part of you whose time has come and we are ready to participate with you on a new level, if that is your desire.

"We can communicate with you at all hours of your day and night. You need only ask for our guidance to receive it. We are here to guide all humanity and not just one particular soul. Each soul is special. Each soul is our charge. Each soul, when ready to connect with us, need only ask for our guidance to receive it.

"We ask for you to share this message to let others know we are available to guide those who wish guidance. We are the White Winged Consciousness of Nine here to help humanity end the enslavement of the soul in which it has participated in for far too long."

ಐ 📖 ೞ

Assure Your Shift

"Relish in these energies as earth continues to change. We the Lemurian Council of Twelve are with humanity, watching, waiting for those ready to make the next shift. This shift shall assure your permanent vibrational frequency with the New Earth into the 5D realm of existence. We are with humanity now to make this next step. This New Earth is already cemented on your planet as all earths, the Inner Earth is now.

"We are with you as you move through your world and we ask that you continue to move through these frequencies of Light carefully to assure your safe journey to the other side of BEing. This state is not one in which many of your people currently exist in but one reserved for those ready to move into the class of Oneness once again.

"Assure your safe arrival by knowing, you are one with each person you relate with; each person you come in contact with holds a key for your further awakening to this class of consciousness. Pay attention to your clues to move into this state of BEing. Pay attention to the movement of energies as they surround you and know you are loved dearly. You are now moving forward as all unseen realms continue to cheer you on. You are becoming One once again and we applaud this supreme effort of will to again meet those parts of your Self left behind so many aeons ago.

"We are here to assist as all watch and cheer."

ॐ 📖 ☾

Higher Realm Messages
~ B ~

Be aware of synchronicities.

Becoming A Correspondent For Higher Realms

"Becoming a correspondent for higher realms is not as difficult as one might think. First, you need the desire to do so for without that there is no way to begin. Second, it is always helpful to keep the host free of substances that might detrimentally affect the host (such as prescription or recreational drugs, alcohol, or other mind-altering substances). Thirdly, it is always a good idea to know that you can channel higher realms at any time, provided you do not question your ability to do so. Take care to keep the body well hydrated for after all it makes the host most receptive for higher energies to come in, especially with the use of salts such as ones used in the world now (Himalayan Salt, etc.). Water is a great conductor to help visibility of higher realms as well but that is another subject.

"Knowing it is all one Source, within the vastness of *All That Is* makes it easy to tap into different aspects of this Source. Although many people do not take the time to ask their Higher Self - - yes, everyone is channeling their own Higher Self from the realm of possibilities and experiences they have brought forth through many lives - - this Higher Self is there for the asking. All in all, it is possible for everyone to channel, on one level or another, based on his or her own experiences in and out of physicality and the soul's plan.

"For those that do not wish to tap into higher realms by themselves, not trusting their ability or doubting the information coming though them, be careful to choose sources of higher quality. By this, we mean, yes we as now we speak in terms of segments joining, be careful to seek out those that do not demand nor ask you to follow their truths. Watch for those that announce their sources are greater than others or those channels that seem to report of the 4D reality consistently. All reports of future happenings in 3D can change based on mass consciousness so it can be difficult to count on any future event.

"We leave you today with these thoughts. Take care to motor through the 3D maze by paying attention to what is around you and if you seek help from others in terms of advice from higher realms check the sources and experience of these channels. Some may be more in tune with your own energies than others may. Know that what you resonant with using your heart may not always match with what you discern with your mind. But using your sixth sense will always light the way, that being how you feel after connecting fully with your Divine spark within.

"It is with the greatest pleasure that we address those in the 3D reality and we are here to help as desired. Yes, we are the White Winged Consciousness of Nine here to assist."

ဘ 📖 ㄜ

Becoming More In Tune

"Connect with your heart of hearts. Remain in that space as your earth continues to change at a rapid rate. You and many others shall lead the way back to Wholeness and Health in all aspects for humanity. Do not be concerned with the rest of the world or what occurs around you. Know that each soul chose its experience before coming to earth and continues to do so to experience, express and expand the richness of their own soul.

"You and many others are now on the very cusp of becoming more in tune with the Light of your own BEingness. This is a lost art now coming into fruition for those who wish to partake of the beauty of *All That Is* within the physical form. Be sure of one thing as these new waves of consciousness continue to come into your earth's field, you are that of which *It* is experiencing life on a whole new level, never experienced before on any realm of existence.

"We are the White Winged Consciousness of Nine here to assist all who ask."

ଐ 📖 ଔ

Behaviors During Energy Downloads: Choose Your Awareness

"Behaviors will change with these downloads of Light, Consciousness/Energy. These behaviors will change with those taking on the Light as well as those not assimilating the Light so effectively or efficiently. Humans unaware of the process do not assimilate the Light as effectively or efficiently. Those not choosing to undergo the process will return to the New Earth to assimilate the process at other times in humanity's awareness.

"Yes, in your small mind of one, all is illusion, as in the Course (*A Course In Miracles*), and yet as you move through this illusion, is it not easier to know these things to help you move through them more smoothly and fluidly? This is the question we ask the channel as she continues to repeatedly question.

"Know, assimilating these energies are best done as discussed in previous channels. Rest is of the utmost importance as is hydration and a lighter diet. The exercise is not as important as these waves are coming though for the body is taxed to the utmost adjusting with these waves. The mineral composition of the body is changing drastically and of course, many are requiring additional minerals, magnesium to be specific. There are other minerals and requirements the human form takes on as these changes coalesce more fluidly on the earth. Each is guided in its own way.

"We, the Lemurian Council of Twelve, will continue to be with those who wish to be guided. Remember, all here now were on, in, the consciousness of Lemuria. The true state of humanity is not a dense human form as it is now; that form is finally moving back to the form we held as true Lemurians. Know that as this process unfolds, those wishing to move though it will move through it with more fluidity and grace when seeking the guidance of their own unique aspects.

"We are the Lemurian Council of Twelve and we are here to help humanity adjust back to the frequency it held so effortlessly upon first arrival on planet earth. We ask you to choose your awareness and to remember that that choice can always be changed. We are One. In Peace, the Lights evolve within you."

ೲ 📖 ೞ

BEingness

"You have been Home. We are with you as you move though this next phase in your evolution. This phase will be the most steadfast; the most true of all your incarnations, for your soul is ready to progress to the next level of BEingness. This BEingness is of your physicality on earth, your soul in other realms and your Essence in *All That Is*.

"This is the time of great evolution for many souls such as yourself. You will recognize these souls by their essence, their energy field, which you shall sense with your heightened senses. Prepare to move on in all aspects as we assist you from other realms of Reality. We are your steadfast team of assistance and shall come through you, with your permission, as the time is appropriate."

ဢ 📖 ಜ

Beliefs, Patterns, And Rituals

"Days and nights upon your planet continue to fill with Christ Consciousness energies. These are the new energies to help humanity move out of the limitation it has placed itself in. As you move through these days and nights, be ever aware of the propensity to hang onto old beliefs, patterns, and rituals. Make room for new beliefs, patterns, and rituals by changing your way of thinking. Move out of your self-imposed box to greater BEing with new thoughts of Christ Consciousness, thoughts of Love, Oneness, and Hope for a brighter future for all.

"We are the White Winged Consciousness of Nine ready to assist as desired."

ঙ 📖 ৎ

Birthing A New Earth

"A New Earth is being birthed. We the White Winged Consciousness of Nine are here to assist those that wish to merge this New Earth with the old one. This New Earth will replace all old corrupt systems and institutions now in place. This procedure will take but few short months but they will be most troublesome for those unprepared for gross change. Allow your Self of One to lead the way as these changes occur. Nothing will be untouched, unchanged.

"We are the White Winged Consciousness of Nine here to assist all those ready to move forward."

80 📖 ෯

Higher Realm Messages
~ C ~

Choose your experience by your
willingness to receive.

Cementing New Earth Energies

"We, the Lemurian Council of Twelve, wish to express our gratitude to those of you moving forward. Gridkeepers, gatekeepers, we are grateful for your assistance in helping to cement New Earth energies. Your world becomes a place of wholeness it once was many aeons ago but this will take some time. In the meantime, we wish to inform and bless all involved in this process, the process of returning to the original form of Light.

"And so it is that we move on knowing the task is achieved for earth is but our path as well. With the assistance of those upon the earth, we move forward in evolution as well. So we thank those stepping forward to replace us.

We, the Lemurian Council of Twelve, wish to salute you as the world returns to its original form, Light. This too shall take many aeons of time. Yet, those of you on the earth now are assisting in this change to cement the process for those to come. We express our gratitude. We know this process is not a steady movement for many. We know this process may seem gruesome and burdensome to many humans on earth. But we wish you to know, it is already achieved in other spaces of time."

ᘓ 📖 ᘔ

Change Your Awareness

"It's time to change your awareness and reconstruct your soul. Each thought plays a role in this process. Each action plays a role in helping you to return to the pristine state in which your soul came to earth so many lives ago. Be aware of thoughts, actions, and deeds and be ever mindful that your world and your soul change with each. You are now foregoing "The Fall" as many refer to it but it is only a thought in the mass consciousness in which you chose to experience, express, and expand. Allow new thoughts of service, abundance, joy and peace to mold your world to reconnect your soul to the state of pristine Oneness that it came to experience in this life. Allow your mind/body to mold back to that pristine state of perfection it left so long ago.

"We are the White Winged Consciousness of Nine ready to assist as you desire. Call upon us in times of need to help you weave through this new matrix of delight and wonder."

ঞ 📖 ৎ

Changing The Habits Of Separation

"We are the White Winged Consciousness of Nine here to help those ready to walk through the portals of greater awareness. Your earth now merges with the Oneness of all life more fully during this your Christmas season. We are with you always no matter the time nor season as each soul evolves to the expression it chose when coming into form. We are here to guide those leading the rest of humanity as they harbor the thoughts of Oneness, of Truth, of Joy for being within physical form and changing the habits of separation.

"It is with the greatest of pleasure that we watch those ready to make this great jump in awareness. We are with you all the way. You need only ask to receive our guidance."

ಐ 📖 ೮ಽ

Changing Systems

"We release you from the bondage you have created yourselves. It is our great honor to help you with this process of being more in tune with your True Self. In coming days, humanity shall see many changes, global, financial, weather and changes in all systems, especially for those in America.

"We are with you guiding your leaders as these changes are made. Do not be afraid of the great changes taking place but know all is in Divine Order as humanity, each one on its own, in its own time, returns to full sovereignty.

"We are the White Winged Consciousness of Nine here to assist as asked. You need only call upon us to get our assistance."

ᚨ 📖 ᚳ

Choices

"As you move though these changes of physicality, know you are watched and guided by those helpful unseen realms. We are with you as you awaken to meet your chosen day. We are with you as you choose to move through that day filled with love or fear. And we know you shall always reap the experience you alone choose to experience. We ask you to consider the best possible choice for the growth of your soul.

"Yes, we are aware that many do not believe in the birth and death of soul thought-forms, for various reasons, but we ask that you become aware that there are always choices to make as long as you seem to be a body in form on earth.

"The vast changes before humanity now coalesce into a mix of ecstasy and agony as all becomes aware, you are not alone in any sense of the word. We are with you as you move though these vast changes and we ask you to consider, 'Will I achieve the soul's growth?'

"We are the Souls Of One here to convey this vital message to all who care to listen. The Souls Of One are a conglomeration of all souls chosen to be in earth form for the purpose of extending the knowledge of Oneness throughout humanity and the Cosmos. We too shall dissipate as all thought-forms merge at the end of time."

ℬ 📖 ℭ

Choosing Your Experience

"You are now on the rainbow of the cusp of leaving this dimension in your small mind of one. Be careful with your choices and know each choice leads to another reality. Choose the choice that resonates for you. Listening to the opinions and judgments of others will often lead one astray but you must use your own discernment and resonance when choosing your choices. You know your path. It is easily followed by staying within your own mind of one.

"Remember, there are no wrong decisions, only choices and experiences. What do you choose to experience? That is your question for today.

"We are the White Winged Consciousness of Nine ready to assist as you ask."

ॐ 📖 ॐ

Clearing Debris From
Previous Lifetimes

"You are clearing debris from previous lifetimes of limitations as you sleep. While visiting these lifetimes it is best to remain aware of your task. You are not the only human to do this at this time and we wish you to know, it is with the greatest pleasure that we guide humanity in this process of becoming more in tune with the richness of your True BEing.

"The days before you now will fill with chaos and confusion for those still living in separation of mind, in limitation of thought and in non-awareness of the True BEing. Those of humanity who have chosen to push through this veil of awareness will not only succeed in their efforts but also lead the way for others to follow.

"We are the White Winged Consciousness of Nine here to assist all who wish our assistance."

ಹಿ 📖 ಆ

Column Of Light

"Your body is a column of Light that needs to be kept up with the pace of earth's changes. You will sense this change as fleeting downloads of Light usually during full moons and planetary alignments. The incoming downloads assist you in tuning more fully to the frequencies of Light that are always apparent but not felt.

"The times on your earth change with increasing fervor and we wish to help you adjust to these changes by offering a heads up, if you will, of the massive changes to come. You have experienced much on your earth but will experience much more. And it is with these Golden Light Downloads that you shall weather the changes more easily, adapt, if you will, more fully.

"We are the White Winged Consciousness of Nine here to assist as desired."

ऌ 📖 ऍ

Cooperation

"Each situation encountered requires cooperation between Self and the small mind of one. You will find that the circumstances to each situation change as your attitude and reaction change. Be ever aware of your propensity to move things in the direction of old habits, old ways of living. Strive now to move all modes of thoughts to new modes of living in greater awareness. This is the way of the future to keep the human vibration high in 5D reality.

"Your world quickly moves into chaos with your New Year but those of you ready to move forward shall do so with a change in thought with each circumstance, reaction, and action. It is not up to you to change the world but yourself as you move through this chaos.

"We are the White Winged Consciousness of Nine ready to assist."

„ 📖 ‟

Creation Lies In Thoughts, Words, And Deeds

"I pray thee that you understand your words, your thoughts, your deeds make your life. This is an easy concept if you only think before speaking. Take back all thought not in tune with the world you wish to see and act as if what you desire is already yours. We are with you all the way but we cannot mold your thoughts, your words, your deeds. You must do this for yourself. We are with all of humanity as these days on your earth continue to change at an alarming rate. Please do pay attention to the thoughts, words, and deeds in your life to mold a better world for yourself and humanity as a whole. Be still and know, I AM lies within waiting to be tapped into at every juncture of time.

"I am Amanda here to help you weave through the maze of earth life."

‰ 📖 ‱

Crescendo Of Change

"You are moving toward a crescendo of change for all of humanity. We are the White Winged Consciousness of Nine here to help you report.

"Humanity now awakens, albeit for some ever so slowly, from the dream of seclusion, limitation and separation from its Source. This is a necessary process for all of humanity to awaken from the dream it has experienced for many lives. All are not yet onboard, meaning those who are ready to work the mines of justice are not yet aware of their role. But in coming days, coming weeks, many more humans will literally awaken to realize that they too hold a role in the awakening of humanity.

"It is with the greatest respect that we watch and guide those now ready to move forward in the process of awakening. We are ready to assist, as always, those who seek assistance from higher realms of the illusion. We are the White Winged Consciousness of Nine here to help those who request the assistance. Stay tuned."

ଚ୦ 📖 ଓଃ

Crossroads

"Allocates to you my dear for moving through these energies with ease and grace. The issues you now face are meant to fine-tune your skills in this regard. We applaud you for moving forward in keeping your vibrational rate. Let us mention, you are again at a crossroads, so to speak, as humanity moves forward to the Light of One.

"Each soul has its own path and each soul will now face the challenges it planned before coming into form. We are with you as you face these challenges, applauding you with each progression towards the Light of One. It is with great respect that we watch you from our point of view.

"We are the White Winged Consciousness of Nine here to assist as you awaken to the Light of One."

৪৩ 📖 ೞ

Higher Realm Messages
~ D ~

Do not be fearful of the days ahead for again they will be gruesome at best.

Deliver Your Message

"We have a message for everyone who joined us in another human life. It is up to us to deliver this message or to receive it from the other human as we connect in coming days. These messages will carry us through the portals of wisdom and Light to make the Heaven on earth we came to mold. These messages are the ones that help us to re-tune, to be more in tune with the energies of earth and the balance of our soul. These messages are helpful to those souls seeking to end their human stint on earth. Not all humans carry these messages at this time but for those that do now is the time to relay them, to seek them out, so pay attention to your daily interactions with other humans.

"It is with the greatest respect that we the White Winged Consciousness of Nine ask you to mold your piece of the human puzzle along with the others to make the world the Heaven on earth that you wish to see."

ઐ 📖 ೞ

Divine Hands

"You are in Divine Hands. There is nothing to fear. Continue your processing and know that all is well. There is a timing to all things in the Universe and your time to process further is now. You will then be ready to embark upon a new path of service and delight, leaving behind the old ways treasured for eons.

"We are the White Winged Consciousness of Nine here to assist as you listen."

ಱ 📖 ಚ

Downloads of Love and Light

"You are receiving these downloads of Love and Light, from the higher realms of your existence, to help you assimilate to the new energies in your earth. Let all things come together as these energies take place and settle in your physical frame. This means to be aware of the need to drink plenty of water, rest as needed, and care for the Host of One in other ways (such as healthy, live food, exercise, and honing the Lightbody). You are one of many going through these changes and it shall become clear to you all that these downloads occur when you are receptive to the higher realms teachings. Rest and know it is all part of your world's evolution as we the White Winged Consciousness of Nine continue to guide."

ଔ 📖 ଓ

Dimensional Realities Separate

"Prepare yourself for a single direct surge, a coming on line if you will. This will be occurring for many in your world within these next few days as the separation between the two dimensional realities further separates. This is a necessary process to help those on the New Earth maintain a more steady foothold in the New Earth.

"You need do nothing to prepare but be aware of the Oneness that surrounds you. This Oneness is the True Source of BEing for all of humanity and shall further cement in your world as chaos and confusion rules for those in the 3D world of separation.

"We are the White Winged Consciousness of Nine here to assist those ready to move forward to the Oneness of humanity."

Higher Realm Messages
~ E ~

Each experience is molded with your thought based on your emotions.

Earth And Body Changes

"As you move through these earth changes, be aware the body changes as well. We, the White Winged Consciousness of Nine wish to convey, this may not be considered an easy process as your systems and organs change to be more in tune with the changing earth. Body heat (caused by changing DNA and increased vibrational rate) signals the mind to know, yes, these changes are occurring. This requires a period of cooling as the body becomes cold. There will be times when one wakes repeatedly to sense these changes.

"Periods of deep sleep coupled with recall of vivid dreams upon waking will signal one in to the differing realities of their own illusion. This is a common occurrence when one begins to recognize the world is not as one has been taught. One may sense other realms of existence in waking hours as well but for the purposes of relating the night experience, we wish to continue. One may experience increased thirst with the subsequent need to eliminate fluid. Yet, the fluid eliminated will always be more than consumed during these bouts of body change so do continue to flood the body with fluid. One may also sense dizziness as the result of traveling between differing vibrations of awareness. And yet, the body will appear 'normal' in all cases. We relate these changes to set your mind at ease; all is well within the process of change for both earth and body.

"We are the White Winged Consciousness of Nine and we are here to assist as always."

ॐ 📖 ॐ

Earth's New Breed

"Allow earth's New Breed to experience their own process as you go through these changes. Their path is quite different than yours and you must adhere to strict guidelines. Do not in any way interfere with their process for it will set you both back in your evolution. They will, as you know, be open to thoughts, but not open to others. This is the way of earth's New Breed, to mold their own frame, so to speak, to be a crucible of Power within her/his self. Take this not lightly but know all on earth serve a purpose, the purpose of evolution, evolving souls to share experiences and master teachings not yet mastered, to move on to other illusions in other worlds. This is the way of the New Breed.

"We are with you always to answer any questions you may have. You need only ask. So be it. We are the White Winged Consciousness of Nine here to assist as desired."

༅ 📖 ༃

Expanding Your Light Body

"Expanding your Lightbody is as easy as knowing expansion comes from within. This expansion is from within the heart's core, the very center of creation itself. Your very BEing is housed within this creation of Love and Light. All now return to this pure state of BEing, if ever so slowly for some, to be in tune with the Self of *All That Is*. Be not afraid of this process as it takes place but know you are carefully watched and guided."

"We are the White Winged Consciousness of Nine here to assist as needed."

    ಙ 📖 ಜ

Experiencing New Surroundings

"The way of life is changing for many people on your planet at this time. You are one of many people who will experience new surroundings on a regular basis to help with earth's movement to the New Earth (opening portals and grounding New Earth energies). This course of events is necessary to help with her passage. You do have a choice, as do others.

"It is up to you to decide how to help with this passage. You can contribute more by remaining in your Self of One but this choice also brings new circumstances into your life. For the first choice, where you take on and live in new surroundings on a regular basis, your soul growth exceeds its chosen path. For the second choice, where you remain in a set location, your body remains at more ease, but you do not experience the pleasures of increased soul growth. It is up to you to decide what path to follow. We leave you with this choice to make knowing there is no wrong choice, only a change in experience.

"We are the White Winged Consciousness of Nine here to assist you and help the planet in the safe passage to the New Earth."

ﻌ 📖 ﻌ

Higher Realm Messages
~ F ~

Follow the path of least resistance.

Fear Not

"You are that of which *It* is. There is nothing to fear. Follow your synchronicities and stay in the flow of magic and Light. We are with you always. We are the White Winged Consciousness of Nine here to assist."

 howl 📖 ℭ

Filling Imaginary Time

"You shall move forward in your quest to help humanity, step by step, as you more fully move out into the world. This crucial step in the soul's work (yes, imaginary as it is) is a necessary step in the soul's process of being and doing, of being and doing the work assigned as part of the Whole of One. Yes, this is a game the soul chose to play before birth. Yes, this is an imaginary game of earth life. Yet, we ask you this:

"What will one do with imaginary time, if not striving to end it with Love and Light-filled camaraderie? What does a human do that is conscious enough to know all is energy, all is affected by energy and all affects energy? One must follow their joy and truth. If one does not resonate with soul's choices, there is always the choice to choose again.

"Make your choices now and be assured it is a game of your making. We are the White Winged Consciousness of Nine here to assist."

ઇ 📖 ଓ

Focus On The Mind Of One

"The Mind of One is open for all to partake of. This state of awareness is a perfect state of BEing that many now will enjoy in 'dream' states. Mind you, a dream is a trip (in one's physical brain) to another reality, another dimension in your time and space that includes your own consciousness.

"The Mind of One is the connected point of reference for all those seeking true Unity. This mind is a true state of BEing where there's no separation. We invite you to visit this space as often as possible as your world seems to make yet another gross adjustment. World events will change drastically in coming months brought on by the ever-changing consciousness of the masses that are now awakening from the dream of separation. This mass awakening will be brought about by what seems to be disruptions in every avenue of life on earth. Those prepared in mind and body will help those yet awakening from the dream of separation.

"Remember, the only way to the other side of illusion is to move through it knowing there is a reason, a season, for humanity's awakening on a grand scale. This awakening will affect all those humans on earth and some more than others. Awakening from the dream of separation does include the knowing that there is only one mind and it is the mind your small mind of one chooses to associate with.

"We, the White Winged Consciousness of Nine, leave you with this thought:

45

"What choice you make as you move through this dream determines where your consciousness lies in other realities of the illusion of time and space."

(In other words, it is time to be fully conscious in all dimensions of time/space, to train the mind to know without a doubt that there is **NO** separation, to focus all thought from the viewpoint of the Mind of One – Oneness – rather than the individual mind of your physicality.

ಬಂ 📖 ಚಾ

Free Will

"We are giving you everything you need to get through this and all subsequent days. It is up to you to use the gifts of Love, of Compassion, of caring for your human beings with the utmost undue harm, meaning no harm at all. We are the White Winged Consciousness of Nine here to assist as you ask but we cannot interfere with your free will, nor your soul's chosen lessons, if you will.

"Pay attention, if you will, to the synchronicities in your life and follow them to reap the best possible experience. We are with you always. Remember, you need only ask to receive."

ଓ 📖 ଔ

Functioning On Other Levels Of Reality

"You are on your way to becoming the person you came (as a soul) to be in this lifetime. This process is in your mind an arduous one but it is only in your mind that this exists. Continue to change your mind, your way of thinking, your perception, to make the process smooth and easy. Continue to look on the bright side, finding the gifts and treasures of what occurs rather than moving to your old way of thinking. We are parts of you still waiting to be incorporated more fully as you move through this process of becoming more in tune with your small self of one, while also functioning more consciously on other levels of reality. We are the White Winged Consciousness of Nine, knowing the process will continue to be a blessed one with thoughts of Wholeness, Peace, Love and Light."

℘ 📖 ℘

Higher Realm Messages
~ G ~

Go forth in the spirit of this New World, blessing all you come upon, for as you bless so are you blessed.

Gatekeeper Message

"Gatekeepers, the time is here. The time to open the portals of new consciousness, new energies, new ways of BEingness is here for humanity no longer lives in the darkness of duality. The time to be at peace with harmony for all is here. The time of abundance and joy for all is here. The time of Oneness is here. Be aware of the ways in which you close these portals of greater awareness by moving toward the duality of darkness. Look upon others as you look upon yourself and know each unique being is indeed a part of the Oneness in which you reside.

"We are the White Winged Consciousness of Nine here to assist those ready to expand the richness of their unique BEing."

ಬಂ 📖 ಚ

Geometrical Shapes

"You will learn to look at shapes geometrically to coalesce all back to the Oneness of all Life. All shapes are designed to be in tune with the Oneness of the Life of which you are. Look around you and see those shapes as you go about your day and know your world is built upon them. They are the building blocks of the Universe.

"We are with you as you shape the New World of Love and Light. We are the White Winged Consciousness of Nine."

ॐ 📖 ☙

Glorious Times Of Grand Change

"The times before you now are the striving of humanity for a better way to live. This way is not far off in your future but as near as the nose on your face. You are in the hardest of times for humanity and yet you are in the most glorious times of grand change as the greatness of humanity bursts forth to be recognized by all. We watch from higher realms as this great change takes place knowing it is already accomplished.

"We are the White Winged Consciousness of Nine here to assist in this change."

80 📖 ∞

Go With The Flow Of Synchronicities

"We are with you. Just go with the flow of synchronicities. The river of life will carry you to where you need to be for this next leg of your journey here on earth. The tides are changing quickly and you must remain in the flow to partake of these greater energies of Love and Light.

"We bid you adieu as you move into your day, knowing you are always, as you know, in the right place at the right time."

"Yes, even knowing there is no time," I hear when silently remarking there is no time.

"We are the White Winged Consciousness of Nine here to assist."

ॐ 📖 ॐ

Gods Of Matter

"All is well my child as you move though these phases of raising consciousness for yourself and that of humanity. It is with the greatest respect that we the White Winged Consciousness of Nine ask you to be more aware of the possibilities that lie before humanity. This is not to say become involved in these possibilities but to be aware they are there for many sleeping humans. Those still not ready to reach higher states of awareness and truth shall become increasingly burdened with consequences of their own making, by giving their power away, by using their free choice and will to allow other, what they believe to be more knowing humans to make their choices for them.

"Much of humanity quickly moves toward these conditions while a much smaller group of humans, awakened to the Truth of BEing continue to make their own rules. Never forget, humanity may be in human form, but nevertheless are gods of creation, with the ability and tools to improve life on a much grander scale than ever before.

"We wish all to know: the Truth of BEing lies inside each individual form waiting to be recognized and utilized for the good of all. There is nothing to stop humanity from this recognition but its own small self of one. Each human holds and must recognize this power held within or succumb to another life on other planets to receive the blessing. Your earth as it is now is changing and shall not be in the state held for aeons of time.

"We are the White Winged Consciousness of Nine here to assist those ready to move forward on the New Earth, knowing ye are gods of matter."

ॐ 📖 ೞ

Grace and Ease

"Be still and know that all is well. Remember to move through this slight period of time with the Grace and Ease that you are. This time is but a short blip on your map of awakening. All questions are answered in time yet be aware there are no questions, only experiences to move through, again with Grace and Ease."

ಹ 📖 ೞ

Grand Awakening of Self

"We are here to share news of your sisters and brothers upon this earth. We are the Lemurian Council of Twelve here to help humanity at this time. We are you in another form, another level of awareness, another state of consciousness and we tell you now, you are all Lemurians. You are all Lemurians from your past lives and this is why you, as souls, chose to come to earth (in your awareness) at this time.

"Many earth changes lie before you. Many changes in the state of consciousness for humanity occurs now and will continue to occur as all move forward to the awareness of one state of BEing, the state of consciousness in which all aspects of the Whole first arrived on earth. This is the state from which humanity chose (as a Whole) to experience, denser and denser forms of BEing. Humanity now returns to the original state of awareness as all unseen realms watch from other states of awareness.

"This event will take some time in the small minds of self, the self of each soul on earth. But be assured it has already occurred. We are here to assist as humanity moves through this process. And we do so in your various states of awareness, meaning we assist each aspect of the Whole based on their current human state of awareness.

"Be assured no one will be left behind in this 'Grand Awakening of Self'. No one will be left to fend for one's small self. You need merely ask for assistance to receive it. We are the Lemurian Council of Twelve here to assist."

 howdy 📖 03

Grand Demonstration Of Changing Energy

"It is all about experience, my dear. You are here to relish in the energies of earth while maintaining your vibrations of Love and Light as earth moves through these times. You are not the only one to experience this grand demonstration of changing energy. All on earth now experience it, whether they know it, or not. The world now changes very quickly for many on your earth. Remain centered in Oneness to move through these times with ease and Grace. It is what you have all come to do.

"Remember, you are God in physical form, playing a game of earth life to experience, express, and expand the richness of *All That Is*. There is no right or wrong. There is only experience and expression.

"We are the White Winged Consciousness of Nine here to assist those ready to move forward in their awareness of Self, the Self of one light, the Light of One."

శ్రి 📖 ℅

Higher Realm Messages
~ H ~

Humanity now moves toward
Oneness at full force.

Help Those Lost In The Maze

"The answers are within you my dear. You have only to pick up the pad and let them flow. We are with you as you move about your chosen dimension. We are with you as you chose to move within the masses. We are with you as you move about the very atoms that cover your chosen awareness, the awareness that you are much more than you have come to believe.

"We wish you to know, there will be great cataclysms on your chosen earth soon. These changes in consciousness will bring forth many awakened masses that will seek out those that know the truth, that ye are one in all aspects. There is no separation among you.

"You must be ready for this evolution of time and space. Your chosen task as a lightworker is to help those lost in the maze of forgetfulness. You know this to be true.

"We are with you as you move about this dimension, but we cannot and will not interfere with the soul's chosen lessons. Yes, all is ultimately illusion. But while seeming to be in the game of time and space it is your charge to mold those atoms of thought-forms to greater realities of love and light, of truth and justice for all humankind.

"We leave you with this last thought. You are relished by all unseen realms as we watch with great anticipation, the beginnings of the last age of forgetfulness. We are the White Winged Consciousness of Nine."

ᘔ 📖 ᘕ

Higher Realm Connections

"Higher realm connections are always with you. You need only take the time to ask your questions, listen, and document your answers. This opportunity is available to all of humanity for the asking.

"We are the White Winged Consciousness of Nine ready to assist as desired by you!"

ॐ 📖 ☙

Higher Realms Easter Sunday Message

"You are coming up to another turning point in life as these energies gather more quickly on earth and in your world of worlds. Let this not dismay nor distract you from your earth mission at this time, which is to alert all on earth that this existence is fleeting at most. You are one of many who shall now move more quickly along the path, seemingly ahead of many others who do not wish to leave the dream behind.

"We are the White Winged Consciousness of Nine here to assist all who seek out our guidance. It is not for us to make your decisions but rather to inform you of the choices that lie ahead. Humanity now undergoes the greatest feat of all history, that of purging, cleansing and transmuting all negative energies it has allocated to thought forms on earth, at this time. Know there are many beings from other states of existence that gather and watch as the earth game progresses. And yes, it is progressing to a crescendo in your earth terms. We are with you as you seem to struggle through your life choices. We are with you when you embrace the new energies and we are cheering you on as you make the necessary changes to move forward on your evolutionary path.

"We are the White Winged Consciousness of Nine here to assist as sought."

૪ 📖 ૭

Holding Lemurian Energies

"We are moving forward in our efforts to assist you as you assist yourself. It is with the greatest of pleasure that we watch you grow and prosper on the New Earth. You are one of many to help the others in humanity to fine-tune their way of thinking, of living, of BEing on the New Earth. The task is to be within the physical frame and yet hold the Lemurian energies of old that many came to incorporate once again during the earth experience.

"It is with the greatest pleasure that we watch our brothers and sisters. We are the Lemurian Council of Twelve and we shall continue to watch over and guide you as you complete your earth experience."

ಬಿ 📖 ೞ

Humanity's Starseed Family

"We've felt so extremely sad these past few years that the world is going to end or go in a direction we do not wish to experience. That time is ending now as those of you who wish to change the earth make the changes necessary to have an earth life that is conducive to good and abundance for all humanity.

"We are with you, your starseed brothers and sisters, as you all come together in this effort of love for all humanity. Our past efforts are now your past efforts as we are One with you. As you move forward into these winter months on your planet, you may be assured of one thing. Change will reach every corner of your earth as massive changes continue to create havoc, the havoc necessary to make your world a better place to live, a heaven on earth, so to speak. This heaven on earth is one you have experienced in other realms, as other forms, and are now bringing into fruition for humanity.

"We are with you as you come together to make these changes. It is with the greatest of love and respect that we watch and guide humanity at this time. We are your Starseed family. We are you in another form, time and space, devoid of separation, and we are with you always."

ೞ 📖 ೞ

Higher Realm Messages
~ I ~

Immense miracles for all of
humanity fill coming days.

In Coming Days

"In the coming days there will be many changes on your earth. These necessary changes will help all of humanity to move further toward the Oneness of which it truly is. These coming changes will assist humanity in coalescing (joining) with other realms. And in turn, these changes assist higher realms in returning to the true state of eternity for all is not as it was since the first human break from Oneness occurred.

"We are the White Winged Consciousness of Nine here to assist all those humans who wish to move further toward the Oneness of all life.

"Beware of your habits, your thoughts, your deeds, and your propensity to move into separation. And be aware that this propensity is the tool that keeps you from evolving back to the True State of One. We are the White Winged Consciousness of Nine here to help those of humanity who wish to become one with Life again. This True State, of happiness, will not occur as long as the human host sees separation.

"Humanity will be tested greatly in the days to come. Let this not dissuade you from knowing 'ye are Gods of Matter' on earth to finally, once and for all, return to the true state of Oneness, never to separate again."

ᔕ 📖 ᔕ

Increased Awareness Of Self

"Pay attention to the people in your life. They are going to change very soon. Many more people will be opening up to an increased awareness of Self and they will seek out those whom they believe will help them understand what it is all about on earth. All are called forth now as these lighter energies take firm hold upon earth. All may not be ready to listen or lead but those that do will be fulfilling their soul's mission on this plane of awareness.

"It is in the best interest of souls to allow each individual to be heard, to experience their own experience and to allow others to do the same. We, the White Winged Consciousness of Nine, are here to assist in that process and we wish those of you who lead by example to know, we are with you all the way. We are here to answer any questions you may have as you lead by example knowing you are not alone.

"On this realm of reality there is a means to increase the state of awareness in which one lives. This is not achieved entirely by being alone (although we do recommend some time be spent alone) but with other humans who can mirror the state of awareness in which you have passed, seek or have meaning to include in your life.

"It is with the greatest respect that we ask you to not hold anyone in disfavor for their beliefs, their chosen experiences, or their particular way of achieving their experience. For know, all souls chose to experience their physicality on this plane in different ways. We, the White Winged Consciousness of Nine, are here to note: all are loved, regardless of the soul's choice to play any role."

൴ 📖 ൱

In The Midst Of Turmoil

"You are moving through this process with the ease and grace of a conscious mind. Do not let the physical circumstances betray you, cause you to think that is all there is, for a vast array of great possibilities lies before you and all those involved in this human drama. We are with you to guide and support but you must take time to listen. We are those parts, aspects if you will, that are on the other side of Life, the unseen realm of which you derive (come from). We are with you now and forevermore for we are One."

১০ 📖 ৫৩

Higher Realm Messages
~ J ~

Just continue to BE and breathe.

Jump! A Message From Higher Self

"It's all happening, right here, right now. Everything is perception, how we choose to see things, what we wish to experience, how we resonate, vibrate, and discern the world around us.

"It's all happening now, all at the same moment. It is all just a matter of changing our vibration, our perception, our free will of choice of experience to jump into another timeline, another point of view, another experience.

"It is all happening now and, as humans, we are afforded the opportunity to amass great libraries of experience and expression through our free will. Be conscious with your thoughts, your words, your deeds, for they do mold your world. Choose your experience on earth using resonance and discernment.

"Do you choose to continue the game of separation? If you do then you shall continue to experience thoughts of separation from others.

"There is no right or wrong. There is only experience and expression in human form.

"The earth experience now, once again, changes to quickly separate those wishing to continue on their journey of separation and those choosing to experience Oneness.

"Thoughts, actions, emotions, words, all play a role in human choices. The thoughts, actions, emotions, and words you hold today shape the timeline and world you live in. Be conscious of the choices you make.

"Do you choose separation or Oneness?

"Do you choose Love or fear?

"The choice is yours (to make).

ജ 📖 ങ

Higher Realm Messages
~ K ~

Keep thoughts positive because
they do create the world.

Key To Dreaming

"What you do from here on out makes no difference in the course of events but will make a difference in your experience. Remember, like energy attracts so to continue drawing in good you must focus on only good with each waking thought, each conscious thought and during sleep as well. For it is during your sleeping hours that this good manifests into your reality more quickly. Get into the habit of monitoring dreams. Remember dreams and place a key to recall it is a dream that can be manipulated. Place the key in each dream to alert you it is a dream and know the course of events can be changed in that dream by recalling that you alone call the shots. You alone are in charge of your world in and out of dreams. Start with the dreams and as you change them, the life you live in 3D will change as well.

"That is what we came to relate at this time. Pay particular attention to dreams. Remember to place a key in each dream to alert you it is a dream that can be manipulated to your liking. This alone will change your dreams, parallel lives and current reality.

"We are the White Winged Consciousness of Nine here to assist as desired by you. But you must listen and record our kind attention to mold yourself a better world."

෨ 📖 ඏ

Key To True Sovereignty

"To the degree that you can accept others is the degree of the unconscious guilt you have to heal. This guilt is enmeshed within the DNA of all humanity.

"We are the White Winged Consciousness of Nine here to help you motor through this maze of delight. We are with you now, and always, to help you make it back to that pristine state of Oneness from which you all reside in all aspects. This pristine state is a state of BEingness that exists on the highest realm of conscious and unconscious existence.

"We are watching over you as these great changes take place upon your earth. Remain calm and know, you are that of which *It* is. There is no need to believe otherwise. Stay in the flow of Love and Light by remaining within your heart at all times. This is the key to true sovereignty, to remain centered in your heart, despite surrounding circumstances.

"We bid you adieu until next time. We are the White Winged Consciousness of Nine here to assist humanity in all aspects of sovereignty and Love."

ജ 📖 ങ

Higher Realm Messages
~ L ~

Live by and allow the Universe to guide you.

Let Go!

"Beautiful soul, you know that of which *It* is lies within you and your experience in limitation is ending due to your efforts to clear and transmute old habits, patterns and rituals. Beautiful soul, your time has come, your guidance continues and all shall unfold in perfect Divine Order just as you know this shall it occur. We are here with you always watching and cheering you on as a human and as a soul in physicality. We are watching as you struggle with faith and tell you now, let go, let go and believe all good things come to you now.

"You need do nothing but allow the flow to place you where you need be. Yes, a difficult concept but you shall see. Let go and allow the universe to guide and care for you as it has cared for those before you.

"We are the White Winged Consciousness of Nine here to assist as asked."

80 📖 ⋈

Lightworker Communication

"You are at a place in the process where all will be known to you soon. Things will change in your world. As these things change, you will change your conditions. Do not follow the old habits, ways of living, unless that is what you wish to experience. You have chosen this experience to help you let go of the control you have strived to keep for aeons of lives. It is in the best interest of all concerned for you to sit back and allow things to unfold. This is not a bad way, or unnecessary process to experience, but something you and the other souls involved chose long ago, before coming to earth for this earth ride.

"Allow yourself to feel feelings that arise, but recall, you are not those feelings, those thoughts, but a spirit in human form experiencing life in physicality. All is well as you go with the flow of life and continue to hold love in your heart. Remember, each person you interact with holds a clue as to what you need to focus on to achieve Life Mastery. Go forth into this New World with the Love and Power that you are.

"We are the White Winged Consciousness of Nine here to assist as desired by your current physicality."

ॐ 📖 ❧

Lightworker's Mission

"Well here we are dear soul, here to again remind you, you were chosen because you are the best soul to successfully complete the mission to which you as a soul agreed to. We wish to remind you again, you are never alone in the Reality of One and that is what you came to master while completing your mission.

"Yes, something new to relate, we hear you. Yes, you are here to master the changing energies while many others fall by the wayside, so to speak, for loss of a better avenue of wording. You are here to master energies not yet incorporated by your soul, and if you allow your ego to get out the way, you shall succeed in this effort.

"It is time to move on to better experiences. Yes, it is time to get the place, the people, the experiences into your life that will bring much joy, much peace, much more happiness than what you currently experience.

"We are the White Winged Consciousness of Nine."

ಬಿ 📖 ಶಿ

Listen To The Voice Within

"The time has come to heal the wounds of the past. This is possible through steady awareness of the Voice within, the Power within the Truth of your very BEing. We are with you to pave the way as you commence to move further into the Oneness of *All That Is*. We are the White Winged Consciousness of Nine ready to assist as desired."

೮ 📖 ೪

Living Alone, Or Not...

"Divine Order and Timing prevail in all things. You need not be on the New Earth or of an increased vibrational rate to experience this. This state of affairs is always present on earth and more so now that things rapidly change for all on the planet.

"Those living alone are alone for good reason just as those in what many would refer to as cumbersome situations are there for good reason as well. All experience is meant to help humanity recognize the Oneness of all things. Treat your companions as yourself and know you alone hold the key to your own awakening.

"We are the White Winged Consciousness of Nine here to assist as desired by all who seek the guidance."

෨ 📖 ෴

Living The Law Of One:
Catastrophic Events

"We are the White Winged Consciousness of Nine with news of humanity's move on this New Earth. The catastrophic events happening in large areas of your earth are preparing the ground for these higher energies of Light and Love. Those humans who have agreed to live in these areas unknowingly are anchoring these new energies. There are those called Gridkeepers who know exactly what they are doing but there are few of them on your earth at this time. Most humans are unaware that catastrophic events help to settle the Light coming into your planet at this time.

"We are here with those of you who hold this Light of One. Yes, it is a light of Oneness that now settles onto your earth. This great assurety of Oneness is for all who do not hold separation within themselves. Remember humanity, you are One. Each person you see, each person you interact with, each person that interacts with you is a part of that Oneness, is a part of you. These are your mirrors as many say. Pay attention to the interactions of your mirrors and know the Law of One returns to earth more steadily at this time. Treat all those you interact with with the knowledge that they are you in another form. They are part of *All That Is*, God, whatever you wish to call it and they are here to help you come into that Oneness within yourself. All those still seeking separation will no longer be supported on this New Earth.

"Now we wish to address those living in catastrophic areas. You are there not only to assist with the settlement of new energies but also the settlement of new communities of Oneness. Reach out to those in need. Build your communities and know all on earth hold a purpose. There are none on this earth who do not have a unique goal as souls. Many may be unaware of this truth and yet each soul holds a unique gift or talent to help humanity move forward into the Law of One once again.

"We are the White Winged Consciousness of Nine. You need only ask to receive the information desired to assist you in once again living the Law of One."

ം 📖 ൽ

Higher Realm Messages
~ M ~

Move out to create in the New World for the foundation is firmly solid.

Manifesting In The Moment Of Now

"*All That Is* awaits your decision to fully participate in the moment of Now. Each now moment brings greater manifestation than ever before so it is important for you to invest your Now time wisely. Focus on what you wish to bring into your life for now the thoughts and emotions of humanity manifest quicker than ever before. Know that you are co-creators here on earth to manifest a better world, first for yourselves and then for the collective consciousness.

"Know that those who chose to participate in this new game will be the masters of their manifested world, manifesting on higher and greater levels than ever before. And know that each human holds the key to their own awakening, for each human chose the time and place of their awakening.

"We are the White Winged Consciousness of Nine here to assist as you ask."

৪০ 📖 ৫৪

Mass Awakening

"Brothers and sisters of the Light awaken to the dream in greater ways than ever before. Hear ye, hear ye all, the mass awakening is upon you. You need do nothing to force this change but remain within your heart, the heart of hearts that is always aware of its very Oneness with all BEing.

"We are the White Winged Consciousness of Nine ready to assist all those ready to move forward into greater ways of living and BEing."

৫০ 📖 ೞ

Maze Of Illusion

"All is well in God's creation, of which you have never left. But here in your world of deceit and mockery it is a much different story as all continue to separate. You are being gifted with the opportunity to remain one with those building strength of character. In this maze you call illusion, it is this tool that helps you to motor through the various passageways of life. This is the tool you and others will use to move through these energies as all others stand inert. We are a part of you in the 4D world assisting as you motor through these growth opportunities. You will re-begin to channel those higher realms when the stresses in your life lessen, to some extent. Take care in the days ahead as all is in a great state of change for all humanity."

ဆ 📖 ಜ

Members Of The Whole

"As we ease into this New Year, let us remember: There are no mistakes, merely experiences to move though, expressions to express, and expansions of the small self of one to E X P A N D. Let us move into this New Year knowing we are on the cusp of being more than ever before. We are on the cusp of becoming sovereign in all ways. It is our charge to change the current state of events as they appear to unite more with the Allness of *All That Is*.

"We are becoming more in tune with our True Nature of Love, of Light, of Wholeness, of Joy, of Peace and Prosperity.

"As you enter this New Year, be aware of the vast multitude of possibilities that lie before you as a member of the Whole. Humanity is but a small part of this Whole and yet it, as all parts, affects the Whole (because there is no separation). You are much more powerful than imagined. Go forth into this New Year knowing the Power you possess to change the world in all ways.

"We are the White Winged Consciousness of Nine ready to assist those willing to listen."

ఠ 📖 �

Message For Lightworkers

"Your empty shell is ready to be filled so be prepared. We are the White Winged Consciousness of Nine here to assist you in this process.

"Each step you take, each movement you make, each decision or lack thereof, fills this shell you call your body. You are at the beginning of the end time for your time on earth. It is a time when things come to fruition for you. Many will seek your help as this world falls into further chaos. Many will seek the advice of one who has experienced what they now do. Be prepared to go the distance and help those who present themselves to you, regardless of monetary payment, for **each task is rewarded with a balance of giving and receiving**.

"We are the White Winged Consciousness of Nine here to assist as you wish and we are with you always."

 જ 📖 ୭

Midst Of Great Change

"You are in the midst of great change. Go with your own resonance and discernment. Travel this road carefully. Remember, your reactions pave the way. Remember, you came here to experience, express and expand those soul parts yearning for expression in all ways. Be aware of it and follow your heart.

"We are the White Winged Consciousness of Nine here to assist as desired."

ൠ 📖 ☙

Mold Your World Consciously

"We are with you always. The task at hand is to mold your world consciously, while living in the 3D reality of earth life. These times on your earth are unprecedented in that they have never, nor will ever, be lived again by any form. The human form is changing to accommodate Mother Earth. This process will take quite a bit of time, in your earth terms, but is but the blink of an eye in terms of eternity.

"Go with the flow of synchronicity, as you would note, and know we unseen realms are with you always to guide and support, always loving unconditionally. We are that of which *It* is, as you and all living things, and we are here to support you in this ever quickly changing process of ascension, becoming more in tune with your true nature. That True Nature is the BEingness of *All That Is*, Perfect, Whole and True. We are morphing forms of Stuff of Matter, here to support you in this journey.

"Namaste."

Molding A New World

"Trust in your ability to mold a new world. Be ever mindful of the thought processes that get you there. There are no boundaries in this new world of your own making. You have everything you need to mold this world of Beauty and Love while continuing your world service in new ways. This is your soul plan to contribute to the mass awakening by helping all to see another way to live, another way to be and another way to dream and exist in this earth reality. Trust in your Self to mold this world and be ever mindful of the thought processes that get you there. You are well loved and watched over very carefully.

"We are the White Winged Consciousness of Nine here to assist all into the new world of wonder, abundance and Love."

Ᏸ 📖 Ꮳ

Move Consciously

"As you move through this day, remember you are in a new state of awareness that offers greater possibilities, greater possibilities of giving, of receiving, of living life to the fullest. As you move through this day, be ever mindful of your thoughts, your deeds, your propensities to follow the old ways of living. As you move through this day, be ever aware of the path you have chosen, the path of service to One, the Oneness of all Life.

"We are the White Winged Consciousness of Nine here to assist as you move through this portal of awareness."

ഉ 📖 ങ

Moving Forward On This New Adventure

"You are passing through a time warp at this time during your July full moon. This will change things on your earth to be more in tune with the Light of One, but only for those who are ready to move toward their full BEingness. For those whose vibrational rates are not yet ready to live in the Light of Oneness, this earth experience will be quite different. Those of you ready to become and remain heart-centered must know this and continue on your own path, while those not yet ready to be all they can be will move away from you and the experience you are having. This is the choice of free will for souls on earth at this time. Each soul chose the experience they wished to have.

"Remember, there is no right, nor wrong. There is only experience, expression, and expansion of the richness of *All That Is*.

"We, the White Winged Consciousness of Nine, are here to assist those ready to move forward on this new adventure."

ഇ 📖 ൃ

Moving Toward Full Sovereignty

"Your journey soars from this point on as you listen while we guide you to full sovereignty. It will be an easy path to follow full of joy and synchronicities, for the time is now here to attune to higher aspects of Self. Help humanity as you help yourself and know we are with you. We are the White Winged Consciousness of Nine here to assist at all times.

"Darkness is all around you and you must find your way by using the Light within. This light is the Divine Spark of One held within you for many eons of time. You, as many others, hold the key to full sovereignty for humanity. And it is with this key that you shall set yourselves free from the mis-thought and abuse of past lives.

"Follow your own resonance and discernment and know that we of the higher realms are ready and willing to assist you."

ഽ 📖 ങ

Higher Realm Messages
~ N ~

Never fear.

Necessary Experiences

"Humanity is under the grand illusion that when we defer we gain. This is not the case but quite the opposite. When you defer something to another time or space you, in essence, are allowing that energy to build to an even greater crescendo. Let us explain this concept.

"Humanity has deferred many multitudes of blessings bestowed upon them for eons of time (by not recognizing them). These blessings come in the form of trials and tribulations to help the planet grow. These blessings are in many forms and may often be overlooked. Humanity always looks for the easy way to live but in Truth, on your planet, this is not the reason souls have chosen to inhabit the earth.

"Humanity has come to earth to grow in awareness of the Truth of One by allowing each soul to experience the necessary experiences to bring that memory back to awareness. Allow yourself to move through these times with the ease and grace of one who knows the Truth. You are not your experience. You are not your errors or even your accomplishments. You ARE that of which *It* is.

"We are the White Winged Consciousness of Nine here to assist as humanity makes yet another great leap in awareness."

꙰ 📖 ꙫ

New Lightbody

"All circuits and pathways are reconnecting in your new lightbody. Take care to cherish and nurture this lightbody in the days ahead by concentrating only on the good things of life. This requires not only good thoughts but also a propensity to follow only your own guidance. Do not be concerned with what goes on around you for your world will be filled with much disarray.

"Drink plenty of water and care for the host in the usual other ways as well. You must listen to the Voice inside to weather this coming course of events for your world now changes with fervor never experienced before on any realm, in any world.

"We are the White Winged Consciousness of Nine here to guide all who wish to follow the path of Christ Consciousness."

ಬಾ 📖 ೞ

New World Of Greater Possibilities

"Go forth into this New World of greater possibilities. We are with you always as this world opens to you to show your gifts and talents, to do what you have ultimately come to do. We are watching as you make each Divine Connection and knowing you are that of which *It* is. There is no need to worry or be upset over current events. All is in Divine Order as you forge this New World and cement your new way of being in Joy, in Truth, in the Love and Prosperity that you are. It is in Divine Order that all happens as it should.

"We are the White Winged Consciousness of Nine here to, as always, assist you."

ॐ 📖 ☙

Higher Realm Messages
~ O ~

One must follow their joy and truth.

Oneness Entrainment

"The energy fields of those in tune with Mother Earth are enlarging. This will help humanity to become One in a most unusual way, by spreading the Oneness and Love through the physical form throughout the earth. You, as a lightworker and wayshower now participate in this loving task. It is not for you or anyone to judge, shame or blame the throes of humanity who are not in tune with Mother Earth, Oneness, or the Love that you are. You are here to experience the changing of the guard and this will, unfortunately, take a bit of time. But pay no mind to those still lost in the midst of forgetting for all are part of the Oneness in all aspects, all forms experiencing what their chosen soul chose to experience.

"We are the White Winged Consciousness of Nine and we are here to help humanity move through this process of receiving more Light and Love throughout the human form with more grace and ease than ever thought possible. We are aware that many humans feel these physical changes but please be aware that this event is unprecedented in your or any other world. The changes you feel help the DNA to change as your energy field expands back to the Oneness of which you really are.

"We are the White Winged Consciousness of Nine here to assist in this effort as many beings in other forms of living watch in great anticipation for the return to Oneness for all Consciousness."

ℬ 📖 ℭ

Oneness Of Life

"All is well. Continue your process of moving toward the Oneness of which you seek in all aspects of mind/body/soul. This is a process that will continue for humanity for quite some time. All those on your planet currently seek this Oneness to be within the Oneness of security, Love and Truth. There is no security, Oneness or Truth on your planet in the current state of humanity.

"Just know this Oneness is a natural course of events of which all are eventually seeking in all aspects of the mind/body/soul.

"We are the White Winged Consciousness of Nine here to assist those who wish to listen and return to the Oneness of Life."

ೞ 📖 ೞ

Open To New Possibilities

"As you open to new possibilities, greater possibilities exist. Keep this in mind as you go about your day. We are with you always. You need only ask to receive. We are the parts of you left unknown waiting for recognition. We are One."

              ಬಿ 📖 ಜ

Higher Realm Messages
~ P ~

Pay attention to those in your direct observance and know they are parts to be accepted within yourself.

Parallel Lives, Clearing, Transmuting And Cleansing: Moving Into The Ethereal Light Form

"You are clearing, transmuting, and cleansing parallel lives to become non-attached. If this is your wish to move into the long ago forgotten ethereal light form it is best to be non-attached to all that transpired upon taking on dense form. We the Lemurian Council Of Twelve know this is not an easy task for humanity. It is because of this that many humans, as souls, did not choose this transformation at this time.

"The non-attachment to dense physical form will take many lifetimes for many humans. But for those few that have chosen to move through this process, in this life, we salute you, knowing it was not an easy soul choice. It is not an easy human choice. And yet, to leave these attachments behind serves the ethereal form by maintaining its purity and Oneness. For recall please, in ethereal form all are already connected, all are already, as you would note, attached. And yet, there is no attachment to singular, separate forms. For in the ethereal form, all are recognized as parts of one another, aspects of *All That Is*. All in this state of being are aware of their unique attributes adding to the Wholeness of the One Thing in which all reside. And yet, as ethereal beings it is known there is no separation among you.

"So now we return to those of you in human form and we ask, 'Is this necessary process yet another movement you as a human

106

wish to make?' Consider your attachments if so. Consider your attachments and continue or begin to free them, to let them go. This does not mean you must step away from anyone in your life, nor in parallel lives. We ask only that you use your resonance and your discernment to attract like energies, for moving into this process will become most cumbersome if still attached to the drama of duality.

"We are the Lemurian Council Of Twelve and we bid you good day knowing your choices are alone yours to make."

Pay Attention

"We are with you. We are those parts of you that have been lost in the maze for aeons of time. We ask you to listen to Self. We ask you to remember, to pay attention to what is on your plate. As things fall apart upon your earth, know that only that which appears in your direct observance should be addressed. Pay attention to those in your direct observance and know they are parts to be accepted within yourself. They are parts to be addressed in other areas of your Self. There is no one here but the Self of each unique individual and each unique individual is now addressing those parts it has cast aside. Become enamored with those parts. Address each part as it appears to you and remember there is only love to be given, accepted and known.

"Continue to pay attention to synchronicities. Pay attention to who is in your life and who is not. This is not a time to reach out. Remember, everything is falling apart right now (and this is an illusory world).

"We are the White Winged Consciousness of Nine and we ask you again, pay attention to what is in your field of energy."

ঙ 📖 ৪

Perfection Is Your Truth!

"Perfection exists in each human form. Each form is unique in all aspects to experience what the soul has come to experience. All souls are only one aspect of One...the origins of each soul within the field of separation. Each soul is unique.

"As each body forms within the field of separation, it takes on a unique personality. The personalities exist with the function to meet the requirements designed by the soul. All personalities are designed with the function to meet the requirements designed by souls. As one moves though this process of returning in all aspects to the BEingness of which it truly is, it is vital to acknowledge the perfection in each form. Acknowledging this perfection not only brings one closer to the Oneness in which it never left but helps one to realize its own uniqueness and perfection.

"Again, we the White Winged Consciousness of Nine relate, each physical form is unique in all aspects of BEing within the field of separation. Each form has a particular personality to experience the requirements its soul has set forth for each life.

"We are the White Winged Consciousness of Nine and we wish all to know, to remember, there is no separation. Although the field of separation appears to exist in the small mind of one it is but an experience of fleeting souls that never were and never shall be. But the consciousness of One, the consciousness of Oneness exists in all realities (although it may remain unrecognized). There is but One and all are part of this One, unique aspects of all things."

&wsupseteq; 📖 ⊂s

Personal Processing

"Personal processing makes Self awareness possible. It is that process that makes it possible, to cause a full-blown break through to Self awareness. You are on the cusp of that process now as you move further into the awareness and BEingness of Self. Be aware of your thoughts, your deeds and actions as you go through the day to maintain the status quo or move forward in the process. It is up to you to be more fluent in the ways and means of Self processing to keep the chaos out of your personal life as you see it all around you.

"Let us focus on the aspects of personal processing as you move though this and everyday.

"We are with you to help. We are the Archangelic Realm ready to assist you as you move forward in your chosen world."

ଓ 📖 ଓଃ

Planetary Energies Of Love And Light

"You'll notice you will get a lot of information from the fall news as these energies of Love and Light settle more fully into your planet. It is not your task to carry others through the portals but to stay open to possibilities and to remain encased in your human form while holding the Light and Love. Please be aware that there are many of you now holding these energies. You shall find yourselves in secure locations with everything you need to complete your soul's mission. We leave you with this thought:

"Be ever aware of your propensity to sway into darker aspects of self and know it is your charge to remain in the Light of One.

"We are the White Winged Consciousness of Nine here to assist in this great earth change."

ৰু 📖 ৪৪

Playing The Earth Game

"As humanity moves forward though these gates of abundance and joy, we the White Winged Consciousness of Nine are with you. We are always with those who have chosen to accept guidance at this time. The treasures of past ages will now be open to you to secure in this lifetime, as you desire. Not everyone will experience these treasures, for keep in mind many souls chose to play the earth game in different ways.

"The ones who chose to experience abundance and joy in this lifetime will do so as these portals of awareness open in their own avenues of thought. Be aware that each soul now moves more in line with its chosen Soul Plan. This Divine Soul Plan will take you all on a journey never experienced before and many will experience gross disturbances of mind and body. This is the choice many souls have made, to experience gross disturbances while others guide (them) having the health, the joy, the abundance needed to do so.

"We, the White Winged Consciousness of Nine, are here to guide as you wish."

ଈ 📖 ଔ

Portals Of Awareness

"The Light and Love of *All That Is* breathes and moves through you and many others as these portals of awareness continue to open on a grander scale. The evolution of your planet continues as all things on your earth continue to change. Let not these changes place you in a state of unsteadiness but allow them to help you secure a new way of living, a greater and new way of BEing, for naught is the release of old ways without a positive change in your way of life.

"Your atmosphere continues to morph as all watch from the higher realms, cheering, knowing the end result of humanity's glorious shift is already achieved.

"We are the White Winged Consciousness of Nine here to assist, as always, as you ask."

ॐ 📖 ✿

Put Ego Aside

"The issues you face are those within your small mind of one, to keep you in this reality of illusion. Yet, you must move forward into the thinking and moving as one, solely with the purpose of seeding a New Earth. Those ready to move forward fuel this purpose. Are you ready to move forward?

"Moving forward into this New Earth requires a belief in the human goodness of your fellow man. It is not based on beliefs and ideas of the past, but fueled forth through the efforts of masters who recognize that **each part of the Whole contributes equally to make the New Earth more conducive to Oneness**. You are ready to move forward in this New Earth when you set your ego aside and join forces with the other masters of Oneness.

"These masters will now join you in the seeding of this New Earth. You will recognize them by their readiness to put ego and Old World ways aside.

"We are the White Winged Consciousness of Nine ready to assist as called upon."

ৼ 📖 ೞ

Higher Realm Messages
~ R ~

Recognize and interact with those
that reach out to you.

Rely On The Divine Spark Within You

"Know that Love is all there is. In this perfect state of Oneness all reside in Wholeness. It is not up to one part of the whole to decide what is right for another but merely to relish in the Love of the Whole of which you are.

"All parts of the Whole of Oneness are within a perfect state of BEing, unmatched on any realm of neither time nor space. All parts of the Whole of One are now ready to assist those not yet aware of their belonging. For in belonging all come together in a pure state of love. Love is the wholeness of One, untouched, untainted, unadulterated by any imaginings on any realm of neither space nor time. To tap into this wholeness of One, rely on the heart space and know the focus on the internal spark within is the only true thing in your world.

"We are with you always. We are you in yet another state of being and we are One."

ಓ 📖 ಞ

Remain Heart-Centered

"You are that of which *It* is. There is no need to fear as you move though these changes. These are necessary changes to get you to where you need to be. These changes will be widespread on your earth and it is in the best interest of all to remain heart-centered as these changes take place. Remain in your heart and know the change you seek is within you.

"We are the White Winged Consciousness of Nine here to assist as always."

ഓ 📖 ൽ

Remain True To Your True Self

"You shall see the glory of the Oneness within as it is your choice to help others recognize this part of yourselves left behind so long ago. You shall do this by remaining true to your own True Self. This is what we have come to remind you of today. It is your charge to be true to your own Nature. You do this by remaining housed within physical form and yet relating to the ethereal realms.

"We are with you all the way as you move though this process. We are the White Winged Consciousness of Nine here to assist."

৪০ 📖 ৪

Remembering Oneness

"Know this, the higher realms lie within each soul, each human to channel at will. We are the White Winged Consciousness of Nine and we are here to assure humanity, you are not alone. You have never been separate and you never will be, but in your earth game, it became necessary to believe this was so while in human form.

"As humanity now moves through this process of recognizing its self, its true self of Oneness, we ask all that are now aware of this achievement of Oneness in all aspects to help those lost in the maze of forgetting. You do not do this by preaching but by being a role model. By showing other humans there is another way to think, to act, to listen to others without judgment or separation. We ask those of you who now are in the mist of re-membering, remember there are no good or bad aspects of anything but merely roles to play.

"Play your role well by knowing and showing, there is no separation; you are the God you seek. You are the one to look up to, each and every human is a soul encased in human form playing her or his role well. For no one is on earth by mistake. We and others have addressed this many times and will continue to do so as humanity moves through this shift in consciousness. There are no strangers on earth, there are no fools, no saviors, no one is here to be held above the other. When you judge another, you are merely judging your own self.

"Be careful to achieve the Oneness you seek by knowing all on earth are gods of matter, here only to play the game of earth life and help humanity return in all aspects to Wholeness, Truth, Love and Light.

"We are the White Winged Consciousness of Nine here to assist those ready to recognize, 'Ye are gods of matter'."

ജ 📖 ഓ

Returning From The Game Of Illusion

"In a land far, far away your soul resides in a pure state of Oneness. Many of you are now returning to that state in physical form. It is with the utmost respect and honor that we of the higher realms watch as you move forward towards this effort. We are with you all as you contain the vestiges of Light within your physical forms to return to this state of perfection.

"Not all choose this state. Be aware of your surroundings and circumstances and know you hold the Light for those that are not yet ready to return from the game of illusion.

"We are the White Winged Consciousness of Nine here to assist those ready to move humanity forward."

ॐ 📖 ॐ

Returning To Light

"For the next 200 years humanity will undergo this process of returning to Light. You and many others have chosen to undergo this process to show others that it can be done and to lead as an example of Light. You all came for this occurrence. You will all undergo this process at some point in your evolution. It is not a process agreed to by much of humanity in this lifetime but more of humanity will undergo the process as time unfolds. All of humanity must undergo this process or leave earth, for earth is now changing herself, returning to the Light from whence she came.

"You will undergo this process more easily if you resonate with your heart rather than your human mind. All upon earth will change in coming days whether they have chosen (as souls) to morph their physicality or not. All on earth changes as these energies cascade from higher realms. All on earth changes as these energies help those on earth (all living things) to be more in tune with earth and one another.

"We are the White Winged Consciousness of Nine here to assist as asked."

๛ 📖 ๛

Returning To Full Sovereignty

"The time is coming for all to be aware of the Light of One. You must put aside your human form differences to do so. This is a necessary task in the process of returning to full sovereignty, to full awareness of who you truly are, spirits in human form, expressing the richness of *All That Is.*

"We of the higher realms are with you all the way as you make this evolutionary change. We are the White Winged Consciousness of Nine here to assist as called upon."

ರು 📖 ೞ

Role Models Of The New Earth

"We are the White Winged Consciousness of Nine and we are here to speak to the role models of America. There are many of you who know your roles well. You are the ones who have left behind all debris of the 3D life. You have nothing left. Your relationships are gone. Your belongings are gone. Your family for the most part is gone. You have no close friends. You are the role models of America and you are here to speak your truth.

"You are One; you are all One and it is time to live by the Law of One. There are those among you who will go to great lengths to prove, to show, that there is none other but One. This will be done by visiting other countries, other areas, along with other states of consciousness. All those within this realm of gross illusion know their role, if not consciously then on an unconscious level.

"Those that are role models are now moving though the fluid stream of 5D reality in the New Earth to show other humans how it is done. It is done by leaving behind absolutely everything you have known before. It is done by setting aside your habits of separation, your habits of the illusion of separation. It is done by moving through the seeming chaos that many see and live through and not being distracted. It is done by knowing that the Universe, so to say, the Law of One, has your back and this network of One is the new reality of the New Earth.

125

"We leave you now amid the chaos of the channel's reality (construction and lawn people) as noise fills the area, with this thought:

"Are you a role model of the New Earth or are you a reporter of the drama?

"The choice is yours. Accept your role and know each human plays its role well, consciously or not.

"We are the White Winged Consciousness of Nine and we are here to assist all those who wish assistance in this new realm, this New Earth, this new thought moment of the 5D reality."

બ્ય 📖 ങ

Higher Realm Messages
~ S ~

Send Loving Light to all space and time daily.

Sensing New World Energies

"Those of you who are going through this process (of awakening) are dealing with these energies now. As humanity awakens, there are these few that will continue to report, to lead the way to change for all people.

"Not all people experience these energies. These changes are not felt nor desired by much of humanity who wishes to continue the earth game as it is, as it has been played for aeons upon aeons of time. But be assured, those that feel and sense these energies are the ones that chose to do so as a soul. It is not up to you to help others with their own unique experience but to move through these changes with as much grace and ease as possible.

"There are many who do not wish to move forward, to go further into the New Earth. These are those who do not sense the changes and those that sense the energies and now wish to retire from earth life. Many refer to these few as great leaders. This changing of the guard now occurs during the next twelve months.

"Be ready to take your spot among the new leaders, if that is your wish. Each soul has free will and although the soul is ready and willing to move forward, it is the choice of each human host as to whether the soul plan will be carried out to full fruition.

"We are the White Winged Consciousness of Nine here to assist those ready to move further into the ways and means of the New World."

☡ 📖 ☡

Separation And The New 5D Earth: Oneness & Separation

"We are the White Winged Consciousness of Nine and we are here to report to those who wish to awaken from the dream within the dream. The erasure of your (3D) world moves forward as all on planet earth sense the energies of Oneness. The Oneness within these energies secures a more steady spot in placement upon the earth of Oneness (the New 5D Earth). The reality of many people now dissipates into this Oneness while those not yet awakened become mired in the disappointment of separation. This separation tears apart all those wishing to remain within it; by this tearing apart, we mean the separation keeps those at a distance from others within the Oneness.

"There is no blending of the two when it comes to families, to friends, to those that know the truth. You many wish to interact with one another but the circumstances within each life will not coalesce. The interactions between those in separation and those in Oneness will not be as strong as days past. The interactions to those in separation from those in Oneness will be, for the most part, planned events, events where plans have been set aside to address those in separation. And yet, this addressing will not occur under the best of circumstances, for those in separation will be hindered with many issues. These issues will keep them in the separation in which their soul seeks to dwell.

"Those within the separation are living within their soul plan and shall remain in separation throughout this lifetime. We ask that those in the state of Oneness know that each soul has made a choice. Each soul's balance will be achieved eventually, if not in this lifetime in yet another. And we ask you to have patience with those still mired in the throes of separation for the Oneness of which all seek lies within.

"We are the White Winged Consciousness of Nine and we are here to report on the steadiness of the Oneness which fills planet earth."

ಖ 📖 ಐ

Serving Your Brothers and Sisters of Light

"Your world is changing quickly and you must step up to the plate more fully. We are aware of your distractions but you must allow these momentary lapses to guide you to a place of full consciousness for all changes on your earth very quickly, very soon. We know you have other things to concentrate on but we ask you to concentrate on your Brothers and Sisters of Light at this time. It is your charge to help them through this maze of earth life. You can do this by offering assistance to those who ask you for advice. This will happen soon and we ask you to do this with an open heart.

"We are the White Winged Consciousness of Nine here to assist as asked."

ಐ 📖 ಚ

Soul Contracts

"As the world moves further into chaos it is time to realize that this is yet another means to move all of humanity to Oneness once again. Yes, for once again humanity has stepped further away from the truth of itself, as one essence in unique forms playing and experiencing a life game on planet earth. It is with the greatest respect that we of higher realms discuss soul contracts today. For this is a necessary part of the much-needed return to Oneness.

"As with all things, one must experience duality in order to tell the difference, to distinguish, between perceptions held by human minds. It has always been this way for humanity and that too is changing as all things on planet earth. But again, allow us to discuss how soul contracts play a role in this return to Oneness.

"Many souls agreed to take on human form to help with this much overdue process on earth's realm. This entails those souls who have agreed to awaken and those who agreed, very gratefully, to take on much darker roles to help their brothers and sisters, those other unique aspects of *All That Is* to remember their true nature. And it is through their acts of anger, their violence and much-needed chaotic acts that the unawakened souls begin the process of returning to the Light from whence all came.

"This process begins with compassion, compassion for your fellow man. And it **is in**

holding this compassion, within the heart's core, that the Divine Spark begins to awaken. Make no mistake, each human upon planet earth carries a unique essence of *All That Is*. It makes no difference what their role is. This Divine Spark is the very essence all have come to awaken during this and subsequent years, as earth returns to its rightful vibration of Light.

"We, the White Winged Consciousness of Nine, leave you with these thoughts:

"If those of the human mind continue to hold separation within them how will the process of awakening unfold? How will those unawakened souls return and remember the Light within if not to experience darkness?"

ઇ 📖 03

Stewards Of The New Earth

"We are the Stewards of the New Earth here to help humanity with the shift. It is with the greatest of pleasure as we watch your world morph back to the Wholeness and Truth that is was so many aeons ago. As this process unfolds, many humans will choose to leave their physicality. We are aware of the great change within the body of those who chose to stay. This body must be cared for with the utmost attention as you morph the DNA to its True Form for the New Earth. Listen to your body, speak with it daily to ask what it needs and know **there are no rules to follow**. Each body morphs to its own time, yet each body that remains on your New Earth will forgo this process

"We are with you to answer any questions you may have. You need only ask to receive. We are the Stewards of the New Earth here to help humanity with this process of returning to Wholeness and Truth."

ᛋ 📖 ᛈ

Storms Of Consciousness

"You have weathered all storms successfully. We are proud of you. The mire of disappointment continues for many in your world but it is a bit of time before the real storms throw your world into future chaos. You are one of those who will lead and help the others through these vast storms of consciousness. For it is through your own experience that they shall benefit. It is but a common time for many to suffer through their own experiences based on the consciousness they hold. Pay attention to thoughts, actions and deeds and consciously know you can mold your world. This is what we come to remind you of on this day. **Mold your world with thoughts you wish to entertain in the New World.**

"We are the White Winged Consciousness of Nine here to assist as you listen."

৪০ 📖 ৫৩

Supporting Humanity

"You can make the journey sweeter for all concerned just by being there, by being the Light and Love that you are, supporting the highest good of all concerned. Remember, it is not about you, or even them, as they appear outside you, but the experience, expression, and expansion of consciousness to greater levels of BEingness, awareness, and Truth.

"You are on the cusp, as many others, of awakening to the Truth of One. All are within the realm of this One, never ending, always expanding Truth of BEing. All are One. All are a part of the Spirit of *All That Is*. There is nothing outside this One. Speak this Truth in all you do and know, you are never on this journey alone for a legion of angels assist you each moment of time and space. We are the White Winged Consciousness of Nine ready to assist and accompany those open to our presence. Namaste."

ଔ 📖 ଓ

Higher Realm Messages
~ T ~

This is the time of miracles and you shall be ready for them as they arrive to help others along the path of self-mastery.

Take Time To Listen

"Higher realms are with you now as you move through the process and procedures of the New Earth. We are ready to assist as needed but you must take the time to listen and ask for this assistance. We do not interfere with free will of individuals nor with mass consciousness on earth. But we are here to assist all those with questions and needs as humanity moves through these portals of health, happiness, prosperity and joy. As these changes take place upon your earth, know that all of humanity is affected. All of humanity now moves through these portals of change at a greater rate. Prepare for increased change as you move through these portals of Light and know we of the higher realms are with you now and always.

"We are the White Winged Consciousness of Nine here to assist as you deem but we will not allow your free will to be tampered with at any time."

῾ 📖 ῾

The Earth Journey

"We are the White Winged Consciousness of Nine assisting humanity to reach higher levels of existence. You need only call on us to answer any questions you may have concerning your journey here on earth. As you know, this is a temporal mind illusion, played out by a figment of *All That Is*, to experience, express and expand its own richness. This is a necessary component of *All That Is* to grow in awareness of Self, which each figment does as it leaves the Source of its BEing to play other games. These games are played on other realms as well but it is only on earth that the game has expanded to one of total amnesia.

"Humanity is now awakening to the truth of its Self as the times on earth change to be more in tune with *All That Is* once again. You and many others chose to lead, so to speak, to pave the way to awareness of True Self, by experiencing other states of awareness while in bodily form. Let this not dissuade you from your own truth. You are Gods of Matter, each precious in its own right, no matter what state of awareness you, your soul, chose to experience or express. All is well on this grand earth game as the illusion continues to change constantly. For some that will mean gross limitation, for others gross states of disconnect from the rest of the world, and yet for others greater, more appealing games to play on other realms of illusionary existence.

"We are the White Winged Consciousness of Nine here to assist as desired. Call upon us whenever questions arise. We are pleased and happy to help with all queries."

ॐ 📖 ॐ

The Path Of Becoming

"You are going through a process where all will be known to you in a short amount of time. This process is necessary to move these energies with ease and grace as your earth and body changes. Beware of the false mind of the self of one that continues to lead you to limitation. Focus only on the Love, Light, Prosperity, Joy, and Beauty that you are and know we are with you all the way along the path of becoming.

"We are the White Winged Consciousness of Nine here to assist."

ॐ 📖 ॐ

There Is No Separation: All Are ONE

"One will seem to experience separation as long as one seems to remain in a body. This state of awareness changes, to a certain degree, when one recognizes aspects of ones self in others. Separation is only in one's mind and each mind, each body, has its own experience and lives within its own universe. Again, each body deals with only its own experience and lives within its own universe, dealing with only the aspects of its own self.

"Recall, all are One and know that as you move though this process, all truly belong and each seeming separate individual in your world is only an aspect of the small separate mind to be recognized and loved for what it is. Love all these aspects as yourself no matter their shape, their form, their experience and accept them into your own consciousness. Recognize each aspect and know that it is you and you are it. Remember, all aspects of your individual experience are parts of your small mind of one to be recognized as who you are. Accept all these parts, all these aspects. As you do so, the turmoil and chaos within your own individual universe will lessen. Each aspect experiences lessons in the avenues of chaos and turmoil but the blessing of Oneness continues on a greater level for those who know there is no separation.

"We are the White Winged Consciousness of Nine and we are here to assist those aspects of the self wishing to return in all aspects of

BEing within the Oneness of which you never left."

ಃ 📖 ೞ

Thought Forms

"The world is changing quickly as these energies coalesce to greater realities, a cleaner earth. Each new soar of energy creates a new wave of consciousness for those ready and willing to share this thought form. These thought forms increase the consciousness of humanity, one wave at a time. Each wave continues to radiate out into the field of consciousness affecting not only your earth but other realms of consciousness as well.

"We are the White Winged Consciousness of Nine and we are here to help all become one in all aspects again, in all states of mind, for all ready and willing to do so. We leave you with this thought:

"How will you change your life as these thought forms permeate your earth with the Love, with the happiness, with the health, with all that is good in your realm?

"As above, so below will be done in your world as you move though these shifts (of consciousness). Watch all as an aspect of self, clearing, transmuting, and cleansing all that does not belong in the 5D realm of reality. As you and others move though these shifts, this will be done."

છ 📖 ૯૩

144

Trust Your Inner Senses

"You are that of which *It* is. There is never a reason to fear. All is in Divine Order as you move through these times of great change on your earth. We, the White Winged Consciousness of Nine, are with you, ever present, to guide along the way. It is up to you to use your own judgment from day to day, as you move through these portals of awareness. True states of BEing are waiting for you and others who take this step to be fully sovereign in a world of your own making.

"Let all decisions be based upon your inner senses rather than depending on outside sources. You are quickly becoming more fully aware of the duties and non-limitations that await you and others as you become the masters you seek. Let all experience teach you the lesson you need to learn. All you seek lies within you. There is no need to seek outside your Self of One.

"We are the White Winged Consciousness of Nine ready to assist as you listen."

ം 📖 ൿ

Higher Realm Messages
~ U ~

Use only life-affirming thoughts.

Use Your Resonance And Discernment

"The waters are muddy. You must wade through them to manifest the life you seek. This does not mean moving into limitation or going into a position of non-resonance. It does mean that you must use your resonance and discernment at all times to assure safe passage through this time of change. We are with you as you build this new life, this new paradigm of greater living, greater being, and greater manifestation on all levels. We are the White Winged Consciousness of Nine here to assist."

ॐ 📖 ☙

Use Your Perception Wisely

"It starts as a failure and then goes to your reflective reality. In other words, once you experience what you perceive to be failure if you feed that emotion, that thought, with continued failure, that is what you will experience in your daily reality. Know this is what makes your daily world, your emotion fed continually with more emotion, which turns into thought. This thought turns into action and makes the reality in which you live.

"When you experience what you perceive to be a failure look at it from a different perspective. Look at it as another way to move toward the success you seek. Look at it as another way not to be. Look at it as another way not to live. Look at it as another way to boost your vibrational rate by deciding to discover new ways of success, new ways to live.

"When you perceive something to be a failure, look at it as experience gained to help you cement a better reality. You do this by concentrating on positive emotion. Positive emotions feed the matrix in which you live with success after success. Positive emotion feeds the world in which you live with the view that you are the Creator you came to be.

"When you experience what you perceive to be failure, know it is just another way to get you to the side of successful living feeding all thought with positive emotion to make the world you, as a soul, came to create!"

ꢮ 📖 ꢯ

148

Higher Realm Messages
~ W ~

What we do reverberates out into the atmosphere to help not only others on earth but those parts of us that are not in human form.

Walk The Path Of Masters

"It is in the surrendering that the knowing occurs. This path of surrender takes one on a trip to self-sufficiency like never before. This is the true path of the master, the one who knows that all possibilities lie in the void. This is the path of many who follow their heart instead of their mind. Know that you and many others are awakening to the path of the master as you surrender to not knowing the outcome of what you refer to as your trials and tribulations.

"We are with you always. You need only ask to receive. We are the White Winged Consciousness of Nine here to assist humanity as you walk the path of masters."

ಹ 📖 ಚ

Wounds And Defenses

"You are moving through a necessary process to get you where you need to be in the New World. This process will bring up wounds and defenses like never before so be prepared to know their value and meaning in your life. It is not up to you to help others process their wounds and defenses but to merely take care of your own by looking at the mirrors as they are presented to you. Ask yourself with each interaction:

"Why is this occurring?"

"Is this something I need to process?

"Will this processing move me further along the path of Oneness without harming another?

"Will it take me back to where I was before?

"Will it move me to new heights unheard of where I can blossom and grow?

"Processing this kind of information is vital to your increased well-being. It is up to you to move through this process with the ease and grace within you. We, the White Winged Consciousness of Nine, are here to assist as asked.

"It is key to not carry memories of past experiences into new ones for they mar the perception of Now. Start each new experience, relationship with a clear, clean slate. Always err on the side of cohesiveness and Oneness, rather than duality and separation.

"Defenses, unconscious reactions, protect wounds. Consider each reaction and determine if there is a wound to be uncovered and healed."

ൟ 📖 ൠ

Higher Realm Messages
~ Y ~

"You are loved beyond your comprehension and entrusted with the keys to a greater future for many more beings than you could ever know. Take care of yourself and know, we are with you all the way." WOW

Your Full Power And Sovereignty

"All humans are gifted channels or would not be on earth at this time. The life you chose to incorporate into your soul lessons and experiences is this one of becoming one in all aspects once again. The time is here to come to your full power and sovereignty. This is a necessary task to help humanity evolve with the New Earth.

"We ask you to now become more aware of the task before you, to see each human being as part of the Whole of One, now returning in all aspects to be *All That Is* in all aspects forevermore. We are the White Winged Consciousness of Nine and we are here to assist those ready to reach this level of awareness. Ask and you shall be rewarded with the tools necessary to move into this power and sovereignty now."

ॐ 📖 ॐ

Your Illusionary Earth Journey

"As you travel through this path just know: all is in Divine Order. You and many others are being led to experience, express and expand in new ways, to lead those behind you on your illusionary earth journey. It is not up to you to help those struggling on the path by interfering with their journey. It is only your charge, your soul's desire, to experience, express and expand your own BEingness as all moves through this eye of the needle period.

"This time, in your earth terms, will last many months, many years for those not aware of Science Of Mind principles, those not aware of those concepts that help to pave the way to greatness in the grand time continuum. Take heart, remain within your heart and know all is in Divine Order as the world and your journey continues to morph. You are that of which *It* is, ultimately experiencing a journey to express on other planes of existence. You are always in your power as a Creator and you alone make your life.

"We are the White Winged Consciousness of Nine here to assist as you listen. We are with you. We are parts of you."

ಐ 📖 ಚಿ

Higher Realm Messages
~ Z ~

Zone In On The Portals.

Zigzag Awareness

"You will continue to make great changes on your earth as these New Earth energies more fully settle into the mass consciousness of humanity. We the Lemurian Council of Twelve wish to acknowledge your and others assistance as all forms and formless beings of Light assimilate greater states of True Awareness, for it is not just humanity that has forgotten its roots but many forms and formless beings of consciousness within *All That Is*.

"As many know, each step forward for humanity continues down the line of remembering for all realities within the time-space continuum. And each forward movement, if you will forgive our use of your human language to assist in your understanding (for there is no forward in Reality), helps all dimensions on every plane and imaginary post of existence in your awareness.

"Yes, it is your awareness that changes. Yet, there seems to be many others within your world that resonate with the great awakening to full sovereignty, full wakefulness of the True Nature all hold within. In your coming days, years, eons (yes eons) all will change as humanity continues to awaken. This is not to be an instantaneous awakening for humanity on a mass level but a slow and more easily assimilated awakening for those forms and formless beings still locked in the drama of forgetting, "Ye are One, in Truth, in Light, in Love, within *All That Is*. It is your very BEing,

157

the very BEing of all form and formless states of consciousness.

"We, the Lemurian Council of Twelve, wish you to know humanity is revered on other realms as this next step in increased awareness moves all into a more steady state of remembrance and remembering."

ﻼ 📖 ﻼ

Zone In On The Portals

"All is as it should be as humanity moves though these portals of greater awareness of higher realms. Flow with the process as the downloads come. Do not fight them or be afraid of them as your body reacts in new ways. Yes, heavy breathing moves one though the process (I hear while thinking about the change in breathing experienced moments before). Yes, all things on earth are affected but only those who chose as souls to be aware of and forgo this DNA change, at this time in the space all know as earth, feel the immense energies to a greater or lesser extent. Move with the flow. Maintain the body's hydration and know you are carefully watched over, guarded and loved beyond human comprehension.

"We are the White Winged Consciousness of Nine here to assist those ready to admit, 'Yes, there is more to earth life than the five human senses detect'."

ᘓ 📖 ᘗ

~ Part Two ~

Author's Experiences

Live a Life Worth Living. Connect
With Source Today.

A Wild And Dizzy New Earth Ride: Frequencies In Dimensions

Dizziness continues to overwhelm me upon waking as the room spins while trying to sit up. How difficult it is to grip walls slowly to get to the bathroom! I am very hot and recall waking many times with a runny nose, watery eyes and bits and pieces of other realm adventures. In one, I taught people about subatomic particles (as if I even know what they are in this life!). Complete exhaustion overwhelms me as it rains periodically while heavy construction, including drilling, hammering, etc., continues outside the building. I cannot get out of bed to rise for the day until one o'clock in the afternoon.

At least the issues – intestinal upset and gas to void upon feeling a pressure within the vaginal area (as the New Earth settles some of us feel this in very physical ways!) – during other very rough nights of frequently rising is not prominent today. Thank God for Valerian Root, which I take 2-3 times a day to lessen that pressure! I also take more magnesium, which does seem to loosen bowels but helps sometimes to sleep better. Wow, what a ride!

"You are moving into another dimension of your time and space. We are the Lemurian Council of Twelve and we are here to assist you. The dizziness you feel is a difference between the frequencies in dimensions. The frequencies in magnetics of your earth are changing more rapidly than ever before. It is important that you continue to ground yourself using Mother Earth herself. You must do this daily. You must walk on your Mother Earth to more fully coalesce with the frequency in magnetics within her. This is your soul's charge. If you do not wish to follow this soul plan you do not need to do so but cementing these energies, more fully coalescing with the frequencies and magnetics of your Mother Earth, will assist you to do so.

"We are with all those now ready to make this switch in frequency. As your earth frequency and magnetics continue to change, many shall experience what is commonly referred to as vertigo. To lessen the trauma of this experience it is necessary to perform this grounding daily. We are with you as you move though this process. We are the Lemurian Council of Twelve and we wish you to know you are never alone. This process is one that has been moved through in previous times upon your earth. This is the last coalescing of energies, of frequencies and magnetics your earth shall experience. This shall take an age as you define it of two-thousand years. This age has begun on your 12/21/2012. Although you may seem human, you are not. You are a soul using a human form to experience through the experience of time.

"We are with you now as you move through this process and you may call upon us to assist you at any time. We are the Lemurian Council of Twelve."

✡

162

After Breakfast Naps

After a breakfast nap, I decide to journal. For at least six years now I seem to feel great exhaustion after breakfast and often fall into a deep sleep. Upon waking, I am aware of having many odd dreams. Perhaps these are parallel realities where I am transmuting, clearing and cleansing all mis-thoughts...

"Your after breakfast naps are a sign of the dis-ease felt between 3D and 5D. As your world continues to change, these occurrences will continue to exacerbate as the body becomes more accustomed to being in 5D reality during sleeping hours. To control these instances, it is necessary to change your thought processes upon waking. Stay within the 5D reality by concentrating only on Oneness, Unity and Wholeness. Do not feel you must change your way of thinking to be here on earth during waking hours. But know you are cared for and need not concern yourself with the 3D matters of support.

"We are the White Winged Consciousness of Nine ready to help as asked."

As I further ground this message, by transferring it from journal to computer, I'm still unsure of exactly what this message means. Extreme tiredness often causes me to lie upon my BioMat and sleep for an hour, even after getting at least ten hours of sleep. I really try not to concern myself with it since I'm alone and able to do this but everyone else seems able to get through the day with loads of energy. Sometimes they get sick, which thankfully I do not, some use caffeine or take prescription drugs that may affect them, but still it seems odd. And yet, when I mention this exhaustion on Facebook many other lightworkers relate to it. Perhaps the only way to get past any doubt is to get blood tests or merely let go and fully trust in the process. Is my ego fooling me into thinking it's part of the morphing process? Will these occurrences lessen as I fully trust, learn how to assimilate 5D frequencies more smoothly and continue to re-enter society?

Sometime after this, I do see a doctor about a double ear infection. He tests my blood because he diagnosed me with severe hypothyroidism years ago but this time all tests come back negative.

✡

Becoming True To Your Mission

A message on September 10, 2014, let's me know I am moving into a new role, adding yet another facet to the diamond of my life!

"And so you begin on a level fully supported in leadership. This is your true state of being to be a leader of One in this world, to be a truth seeker, to be one who follows the rules of the game but also merges those rules with those of ancient times. You are ready for this move to a New Reality. Let all else fade away as you take on this new role knowing, you are fully supported by those realms you refer to as 'Higher'.

"This is your mission here, to be fully supported as you lead others to the safety and security of their own BEingness. This is your true soul plan to lead those ready and willing to their true sovereignty, to be within their own truth and know that they too are fully supported.

"We are with you as you travel this path. We are with you as you make new ground in this endeavor of becoming true to your mission. We are with you always as one part of the Whole of *All That Is*. It is with the greatest honor that we lead you as you lead others. Be aware of thoughts, words, actions, and deeds on a new level of awareness as all else fades away.

"We are the Keeper of One here to assist you in this New World."

✡

Beings Of Illumined Truth

"Taking time to document messages from unseen realms is merely a matter of setting aside the time to do so. There are many important messages for you to gift humanity with and we, the Beings of Illumined Truth, will impart them to you in due time.

"We are fully aware of the grieving process of a mother who has seemingly lost a child and shall allow you this time to grieve. But make no mistake; your work here on earth is yet to be complete. We shall guide you all the way assuring you have what you need to exist on this realm with everything you need and more, as you have become accustomed. We leave you with this thought:

"What will you do when the time comes for you to merge more fully with your multidimensional Self on this earth?"

This message came not quite a month since Wendy took her own life. Days later, Wendy seemed to communicate soul messages for humanity and myself, most of which are now in *After Death, Communications...WOW!* It is now Fall of 2018 and I still do not set time aside to channel regularly. But my living situation is very much improved and I am in a place where I need not worry about survival needs as much as before. And connecting with my multidimensional Self is a much easier daily occurrence.

✡

Blending In With Dissimilar Energies

After screaming in my new pillow, while lying on my new queen-sized bed – in my new living space (yes again), I sense a message and take the time to document it.

"You are coming to a point in your evolution where things will move much more quickly, much more smoothly, as you adhere to the energies around you. We realize, for a human, these discarnate energies – in your mind – may not always be so tasteful, so to speak. But we ask that you continue to recall, all on your chosen earth realm, all in your chosen illusion, is but illusion, illusion of your own soul to complete many incarnations.

"This is your key, to know, this is, if you so choose, your last life cycle on Earth, your last life cycle in human form. This will carry you through the maze of forgetting.

"We the White Winged Consciousness of Nine wish to inform you these discarnate energies – in your mind – will dissipate as you merge with them, recognizing them as aspects of the experience and yet aspects you continue to hold within. For all is within and without you. You are your own universe, your own multiverse, your own galaxy, etc. Pay attention to the reactions and continue to respond rather than react.

"We, the White Winged Consciousness of Nine, wish to relate, we know how difficult a human form feels as it moves through the process of becoming one with *All That Is* again and we wish to thank you for your efforts in becoming the best human you can possibly be.

"We bid you farewell with this reminder, we are you and await your queries at any time."

Yes, moving again (after being in a place for only eight months) seemed difficult but Divine Order and Divine Timing prevailed. Despite once again being forced to change my perspective, the positive circumstances of my new space were unsurpassed. With loads of my own grunt work and a bit of family and friends efforts, the new space now holds very few belongings and nothing left from a life once dearly savored.

✡

Beware the Straying Mind

Words wake me at dawn on Sunday. Sometimes I just do not want to wake to record them but this time I ask for the sentence to repeat while I grab my bedside recorder to document the message.

"Beware the straying mind that keeps you locked in the illusion of time and space. This world is of your making and truly a space of time wholly centered on your thoughts. This is the state of affairs you have come to correct, if we may use your language, to correct in that it is not of a time and space atmosphere from which you hail (come from).

"These thoughts keep you in the illusion by straying from those thoughts that will set you free from the maze of illusion. It is in your best interest, and the best interest of all, to remain centered, to remain within your own field of Self, to keep on the path of Truth and Light. To do this, remain calm and think of nothing but the beauty and perfection of your heart center. Focus on the heart center and know it is the key to remaining within your own Truth as these days continue to change at an alarming rate. Be aware of your thoughts but let them pass through you as they come. Acknowledge them but know they are just a distraction from the real course of events that never changes.

"Your thoughts change continually but your True State never changes. Be aware of this fact and keep centered in your heart.

"We are the White Winged Consciousness of Nine here to assist you as you desire to be assisted."

✡

Channel The Light Of One

"It is of the utmost importance to channel the Light of One as your earth moves through these energetic changes. Much separation continues to play out in your world. The Oneness in which all live in Truth is readily available for those that know of it. We are the White Winged Consciousness of Nine and we are here to help those within this Oneness devoid of separation.

"The truth of your BEing is One, one Truth, one Light, one Life in which all unique aspects of the Whole reside. Know that as your earth moves through these energetic changes the chaos of separation increases for those choosing not to experience Oneness. Yes, it is a soul choice. And please recall, there is no right nor wrong in your world. Each soul chooses each life experience before birth and each soul experiences the choices of that soul plan using free will and choice.

"Many humans are not yet ready to return in all aspects to the Oneness in which each unique aspect of *All That Is* truly resides. Know that as your earth changes this separation will continue to be more rampant.

"It is of the utmost importance for those experiencing the Oneness of *All That Is* to continue to draw in the Light of One as these energies permeate your earth. Each human is guided in their own way. Know that as these energies continue to permeate your earth all are guided within this Oneness of Light to take in this Oneness, take in this Light, to maintain

171

and increase the vibrational aspects of the Whole of One.

"Know that as your earth changes we of the unseen realms are here to help all those wishing to hold within and reflect, and radiate, this Light of Oneness. We leave you now with this blessing:

"You are loved beyond your human comprehension. Guidance of unseen realms continues to support all those reflecting and radiating the Oneness of Truth."

There will be times when one awakens, still on the cusp of sleep, sensing they are receiving downloads of Light. This light is best assimilated when acknowledged and accepted as downloads occur. Upon sensing this light coming into the crown charka, envision it moving down the spine to the feet and back up again in an arc on each side outside of the body to again join with the stream of Light coming from unseen realms, seeming to be above ones head and body. Continue this process for as long as comfortable knowing that all have not left the state of Oneness. Yet, each plays it's own game within this illusion. The next step is to radiate the Light held within to the world and beyond.

✡

Clearing Aspects Of Self

"There are nine aspects of Self to clear and cleanse in this lifetime for you. You are on the cusp of awakening to a brand new beginning as these essential aspects are cleared and cleansed. We are with you as you take the time and effort to clear these mis-guided thought systems from your area of existence. Know that each aspect is but a part of you left from eons ago that found..."

The words seem to stop so I fall back asleep only to wake again upon hearing aspects of Self to clear and cleanse. The ones I heard were:
- Looking outside your Self
- Limiting your Self
- Devaluing your Self
- Creating distractions from your soul plan
- Negating your gifts
- Repeating your experiences
- Avoiding the truth of Oneness

My brain then repeats an affirmation to clear and cleanse these aspects but I do not rise to document it. More words come when the affirmation is complete.

"You are a Powerful Creator with the ability to manifest a New World. Go forth and use your powers to manifest this world now."

✡

Commit Fully

A rest period from 11:45-12:15 takes place and upon waking, I open to guidance as to why naps/rest periods seem necessary on some days. Is it underlying depression? Is it a physical mis-alignment? Is it emotional? Can I ignore the tiredness and do constructive work/exercise instead? It seems as if I've tried this but it just delays the nap/rest period.

As long as I am able to live as I please, it seems a mute point but thoughts of living by someone else's schedule to make a living rise as...

The White Winged Consciousness of Nine begins to communicate with me.

"It does not matter what you do. The key is to commit fully to any endeavors. Allow the energy to flow freely by maintaining thoughts in one direction. There are no buts, no right, no wrong. Remember, all is experience of the soul. Your soul chose to experience this life with trust, in later years, of the abundance and flow of good maintained through constant positive thought. It is up to you to maintain this thought.

"We leave you now with these words:

"Trust in the Oneness of all life to carry you through this process as it evolves more fully.

"We are the White Winged Consciousness of Nine here to assist as desired."

While wavering and getting ready to move in with a kind stranger, after nearly five weeks of wondering where to go, I finally transcribe this message onto the computer seven months after receiving it. Yesterday a speaker at the Theosophical Society of Deerfield Beach, Florida reminded us of the power of words and thoughts. I have been affirming my propensity to remain within the God Network and be led to the right and perfect place. Of course, this occurs even as I do the work of looking outside what I believe to be the God Network, by seeking ads and checking out non-resonating spaces.

✡

Commodities

Rain falls from gray skies as I wake to recall a dream in which one of my beloved brothers was again homeless. A message comes as I ponder the dream.

"It is up to you to be aware of the possibilities but to not feed any of those possibilities with your thought. Remember, in this New Earth, your thoughts are the most precious commodity of all. Many have other commodities to get them through these times but it is your thought, your ability to shape your own destiny, which shall carry you through this new maze.

"We are the White Winged Consciousness of Nine ready to assist as always. Call upon us in times of need."

✡

Contract With The Forces Of Creation

"We are the White Winged Consciousness of Nine here to inform you, to assist you on your journey. Your world changes quickly in these coming days. It is not up to you to alert anyone but yourself. It is time to step up your soul's work. That is why all of your human distractions are now removed. We are here to remind you of your soul's plan, your contract with the forces of Creation. As a soul, you chose to play a bigger role during this planet's transition to Light. We are reminding you of this role now. It is in your best interest to remain reaction-free as things move forward. Remember, **each reaction merely feeds the circumstance**. We are the White Winged Consciousness of Nine here to assist as asked."

This message came two months after Wendy's transition. Even knowing all contracts are now null and void and this is really a game played by souls, I continue to choose to assist humanity.

✡

Darker Aspects Of Soul

As dusk falls, the White Winged Consciousness of Nine delivers a much appreciated message reminding me that everyone I interact with is a part of me. I am to consider their words and actions, see if I am experiencing, or have had, similar words and actions, and act accordingly. I can clear any remaining wounds and defenses this way and also seem to help what appears outside myself by sharing, as appropriate, and allowing as needed.

"It is all in the listening that we connect with our Self. The listening is vital to interact with those lost parts of Self that are now ready to be recognized and received with Grace and Ease. Be not afraid of the darker aspects of Soul but know these too are part of the earth game.

"We bid you good night on the eve of great awakening for all."

✡

Energy Balancing

So much to relate but there's no desire to do so. I will note what came to me several days ago while pondering dialogue for a client.

"Long ago, in a place called Lemuria, we had the ability to maintain perfect health. Those days are gone but we now possess the ability to reclaim health through energy balancing. There are many ways to do this through sound, movement and color."

We are finally moving back to these tried and true methods of keeping the body healthy and whole. Consider sound, movement and color when weighing healthcare choices.

✡

Erased Memories

"We continue to help humanity transmute, cleanse and clear parallel lives and people not in the highest interest of the soul. Each life lesson, each life journey is now registered in the Akashic Record of the soul and therefore the tools used to reach these heights are no longer necessary. These tools (people, conditions, etc.) are now being erased from the memories of those who have chosen as souls and consciously as humans to move forward into the new timeline of Gaia. It is in the best interest of each human to take the time to repeat:

"I now with Grace and Ease clear all that is not in the best interest of my soul plan. I now with Grace and Ease fully accept my sovereignty and move forward to the New Earth free of all limitation."

"We are the White Winged Consciousness of Nine here to assist those ready to move forward."

Now it's clear that the people and conditions in this life that do not align with those of us holding New Earth energies (not in the interest of Oneness or the highest good) fall further away from our energy field. This is something I've experienced during the past several years.

✡

Ethereal Forms

"We are ethereal forms in essence, in Truth, in Light. This form is merely a stones throw away for those in your world who have chosen to return to the essence of BEing, as originally experienced in this realm of earth.

"Many forms now take on more denseness of earth as great changes, cataclysms, change the shape, the form, the consciousness of earth. Many humans are not yet aware of the truth of BEing. These humans shall continue to experience greater aspects of the denseness of humanity's choice to leave ethereal form. This ethereal form will be unavailable to those living in separation, for only those remembering the Oneness first experienced in form upon earth will return to this original Light Of One.

"Recall the Light Of One was not dense. The Light Of One contained all of those unique essences, aspects of *All That Is* desiring to experience life in other richness of BEing. And yet, many of these aspects chose to not return to the Light Of One until all experience balanced in a manner where the experience was sought, experienced and balanced. This meaning all Light and all darkness experienced by those wishing/desiring to experience the Oneness in other aspects of BEing.

"We, the White Winged Consciousness of Nine, are with you now as many chose to return to the Light Of One. This possibility is greater upon remaining within the non-separation of thought. Most thought forms on your earth full of denseness will continue for people not desiring the Oneness of all life. We shall leave you with this Truth:

"All are One; all exist within the continuity of One. All exist within the realm in which all experiences return to the Oneness of the Light Of One."

Construction continues in my new very affordable apartment as wonderful Cuban crews from Miami replace out-dated, worn windows with hurricane proof panes. The noise can be deafening. As this channel came though the pounding began and continued in buildings next door but thankfully, this channel has learned to deal with distraction. The past two nights have been very arduous, with many vivid dreams and going back into some of these seeming parallel realities to balance events. This in addition to waking repeatedly to urinate and sip more water, massive body aches and pains, feeling extremely hot and then very cold, runny nose, sensing ear drainage and the rest of it. Yet, I am so very grateful to be conscious of what seems to be occurring and to again be in my own space and able to consciously evolve as a human and soul!

✡

Evolution

Things are getting better, yet at times, I long for someone of close mind to discuss things with and share the time with when not working. Wendy comes to me at dusk while I think of her. And I know she is just a tool my little self uses to allow me to tap into a higher state of awareness...

"Momma, I am always here, in your small mind of one. You know it is not a mind at all but an energy field that is slowly but readily leaving as evolution continues evolution of your mind/body, evolution of planet earth and evolution of humanity upon her. Yes, it is a thought system left unattended for a very long time and that is what we can discuss today.

"This thought, evolution if you will, is necessary for each human on planet earth in order to help humanity leave its current state of sleep, the sleep of the unawakened, unawakened to the true state of all things real.

"There is nothing real in this mind/body thought system and this is your charge, as you know, to hold this steadfast thought and carry it to all you interact with at all times. This will not be easy in coming days but remain calm and know it is a thought system that is now being taken on by many more human mind/body thought forms than ever before. And yes, you hold these thought forms within you. It remains in your best interest to stick to yourself and you are gifted with the necessary 3D tools to now accomplish this without causing undue stress to the emotional field of the mind/body system that you seem to inhabit.

"Know, we of higher levels of awareness, other separated parts of your own BEing, are always near and ready to guide as you tap into these energy fields of your own consciousness. Yes, each human holds this ability but few are able or willing to tap into it to reap the tools they need to awaken from the dream. Yes, it is all experience, expression and expansion of the individual, seemingly separated soul. And this too shall dissipate when all thought forms, all mind/body systems come together as in the beginning of the separation period. This too shall pass as *All That Is* finally becomes recognizable to all mind/body thought forms."

✡

Expressing The Divine Spark Within

As I begin to write dialogue for the marketing video to launch my new production company, SAM I AM PROductions, a message comes.

"We follow you at will as you seek the Divine Spark within and know all is well in the realms that assist you. Do not be fearful of the days ahead for again they will be gruesome at best. But you will surpass all expectations with all efforts to express the Divine Spark within. It is your soul plan to help others express their Divine Spark and you shall, as expected and realized, do this work though the production company you now develop. Let us fill the gaps in time with words for you to consider:

"All lies in readiness for your arrival on higher realms of awareness. It is within the bounds of your world to now readily morph all awareness to that of the fifth dimension, if you so choose. It is in the realms of expectation that many will follow this path to end the eons of gross misuse of your planet and understanding of your true nature. We are with you as you pave the way for others to follow the path of Oneness for in Reality there is but one life within which you reside in all form and manner.

"We take our leave knowing the work you now persist in achieving is already accomplished. We are the White Winged Consciousness of Nine here to assist as desired. Call upon us at will for each question or query that arises."

I am knowing all is in Divine Order.

✡

Fear

Current events make things very clear while pondering the personal and financial disclosure dilemmas of firestarter.com (a website designed to help people seed a new business). I continue to be prompted to face all fears, to move beyond the limitations of 3D thought and know the Universe, *All That Is*, God, whatever one wishes to refer to It as, has my back and I am being carefully watched and guided. The donation website requires massive personal and financial disclosures, required by Amazon, in order to accept donations (social security number, bank account number and other normally personal information). This situation is just another thing that I put into the mix to break through my fear. I have avoided being "on the grid" and entering all personal/financial information onto the Internet in one place. But now, as *A Course In Miracles* student, I realize, it's okay to disclose everything for there is nothing to fear but fear itself. My thoughts and beliefs will always manifest so as long as I do not focus on negative aspects they will not occur. And now a message flows quickly from head to hand...

"Fear is an intangible thing created by humanity to keep one locked into 3D reality. Humanity is now breaking through all the barriers it placed on itself so long ago. Breaking through these barriers is a necessary step to move back into the lighter, more life affirming, energies that now permeate the planet.

"You and many others are facing the fears your soul put into the earth game to eradicate all mis-thought. Move through these times with Ease and Grace knowing the only thing to fear is fear itself. You are unlimited beings with the ability to manifest your ideal world. You are doing that now and we are proud to stand by as this monumental change takes place.

"We are the White Winged Consciousness of Nine here to assist as all ready themselves for the greatest cataclysmic change of all time and space, the return to total sovereignty."

✡

Focus On The Bigger Picture

My beautiful sister Sarah (in the books) will be going in for her second heart surgery in two months (she breezed through the surgery again). Either they screwed up the first time when placing the heart fibrillator in her or it went haywire when her power went off for a short time during Hurricane Irma. In any event, a wire came loose but I am grateful she feels no pain. Again, she is scared and again I have tried to alleviate her concerns, but still dealing with Irma's aftereffects myself I am hesitant to travel the four hours to see her. Now, I ask for guidance.

"It is not your charge to be in the drama (another persons drama). It is only your charge to hone the vibrational rate within you. Remember, you are helping many more people with your gifts, talents, propensity to see the bigger picture. Yes, as a human you wish to support and love those close to you. But let us be clear, your task is to complete your mission of letting and allowing, letting as many people know of the bigger picture, allowing those still lost in the drama of 3D to have their chosen experience.

"Yes, you can and will help those lost in the dream in a much bigger way by allowing them to complete their journey of one small soul seeking experience, expression and expansion through areas not yet experienced.

"We are the White Winged Consciousness of Nine and will continue to guide you but you must continue to focus on the bigger picture. We know as a human, you wish to be with those human loves/loved but the picture for you is much greater now. You have all you need to continue your journey of Love/Light. You will be given opportunities to take and it is with the greatest honor that we ask you to always consider the bigger picture of One."

Now I decide to purchase and mail a talking inspirational card to lift Sarah's spirits. She will get the card before her surgery when mailed today.

✡

Going With The Flow

"How can I be a better person?" I ask my Higher Self.

"To start, begin by getting out of your own way. Go with the flow, follow the synchronicities and when there are none get out into the world to create them. Yes, synchronicities are part of the God network that thing that keeps all of humanity hooked up to one another.

"Be clear about one thing. You are never alone. It does not serve you to think or believe that you are. A realm of angels and guides goes before you to pave the way. But you must listen and follow your intuition and, yes, you must hone your intuition but most importantly you must be open to listening and that means taking time out from your day, at least once a day, if not more, to ask questions that concern you and receive answers to those questions.

"What do you wish to know?"

"When will I get the place I desire? Will it indeed be in a private home?"

The energy seems to change now to the White Winged Consciousness of Nine.

"The place, as noted earlier, is already there for you. As you open to change, it becomes more available to you. Yes, as you believe, Divine Order and Divine Timing do prevail but this is something that also must be well planned in the physical world. By this we mean it must be paved, a way must be paved by physical forces to accompany you to that location. And so follow your instincts, take the time to listen and stay in the flow of the group of angels with which you travel. These angels are in physicality and in your life for a reason.

"You have placed these people in your life for specific purposes and now you see that the homeowner's purpose is nearly complete in your life. Yes, it is time to move on and soon. There will be glaring opportunities for you to do so in this coming week. But be forewarned these opportunities will also take you out of your comfort zone. That is the purpose of your last twenty years, your life in general to take you out of a comfort zone and to be able to withstand the massive earth changes to come as you help others through them.

"Yes, as suspected, you are one of many to help others with the changes to come and it is through your experience that you shall be qualified to do so, not by some educational degree but by your personal experience.

"We leave you now, the White Winged Consciousness of Nine, to listen to your soul and do what gives you joy."

Months later, I do move to what seems the perfect little private cottage. Intuitively, I know the move and cottage owner are part of my soul's contract even though I am out of my comfort zone for much of the short time there.

✡

Golden Light Downloads Terms Of Use

A message breaks through the veil at 4:40 AM after a rough night filled with intestinal upset and upper body heat followed by bouts of feeling very cold. I wake aware of lucid dreaming, having a dream inside another dream where I flew through the sky. Yes, another dimensional reality in which my unique figment of One holds higher energies more in tune with *All That Is*!

- "Send Loving Light to all space and time daily.

- "Use only life-affirming thoughts.

- "Care for the physical host with the utmost attention.

- "Be kind to your fellow man/woman.

- "Bear the Light of One in all circumstances and remain within your own Self of One as this earth changes rapidly to become the Garden of Eden it once was.

"These are the *Terms of Use* for your daily Golden Light Downloads. Please spread the word they are to be adhered to in all circumstances, for it is a privilege to sense and feel these downloads from Home. They are not to be taken lightly for they assist you in adjusting to new energies.

"We are the White Winged Consciousness of Nine here to assist all who are ready to move forward."

The intense energy dissipates and my breathing changes. I am very thirsty while running to the toilet. Yes, there are sometimes unwanted consequences to receiving downloads of Light or messages from what seem to be higher dimensional realms!

✡

Growth Spurts

"Growth spurts offer an opportunity to move forward in your evolution by helping you to let go of the old ways and habits that hold you back. Humanity now goes through these periods of growth spurts at much faster rates. You are one of many experiencing these spurts as the earth undergoes massive change. **Be ever aware of the fact that many do not follow your path and do not share your experiences with those not choosing to move along this new evolutionary path at this time.**

"All will eventually move through this path but not in their current lifetime. As noted earlier (in previous channeled messages) not all have chosen to leave the 3D game of experience, expression, and expansion. The ways of old now struggle to stay in place and during this time of great change will try to make it increasingly hard for those on earth. Do not succumb to the heightened drama around you but remain in 5D reality by watching your reaction to circumstances for **each reaction leads you to a different outcome and path of reality in your world**.

"We are the White Winged Consciousness of Nine ready to assist those ready to continue this new evolutionary game."

This message came after garbage men performing their task on Thanksgiving Day jostled me awake. Upon grounding the message into this reality, by documenting it and reading it, I realize it is a heads-up of today's events. Family interactions always offer enormous opportunities to practice my skill of remaining in 5D reality.

Thank goodness sleeping is much deeper and longer during the night. Last night's sleep was even more satisfying than usual for I woke only two or three times during a 6½-hour period, quite a change from years of waking repeatedly after mere minutes of dozing.

Notes On Changing Habits...

Habits can keep us in limitation or soar us to unheard of heights. We need only to pay attention to them to prosper and grow. Staying within the same mindset keeps us in a limited scope of life, making it hard to jump timelines into other realities. We achieve greater ways of living by moving out of our comfort zones. This takes a bit of doing so it's always easier to start small by changing little habits of daily life.

It is only through the habit of assessing daily routines that we grow to become more of what life has to offer. Let us start by changing small things. If one is accustomed to washing their hair before the rest of the body during a shower wash the body first and the hair last. Change the daily routine of buying expensive coffee on the way to work. These are simple ways to start and become accustomed to changing limiting habits. By remaining true to our nature of change, we reach the pinnacle of happiness, health and wealth.

✡

Housing Decisions

Once again, while pondering whether to rent a room from someone who I do not fully resonate with, the verification needed to move forward comes.

"There is no right, no wrong. There is only experience, expression and expansion. Which choice will assist you in expressing and expanding? That is the question you seek to answer. We cannot guide your decisions in other ways but we can afford you the knowledge you seek to make your decision. Your soul chose to expand to the highest degree possible in this life. It is a brave choice made by few souls who wish to end the game of limitation. Of course, this can mean living in limitation to some degree, if only as a learning tool. What do you wish to experience? That is the question to answer as you seek housing in coming days. This is the choice of many souls now at this juncture in time.

"We are with you always. You need only ask to receive. We are the White Winged Consciousness of Nine here to assist."

Yes, it is a choice of experience and expansion, and living with someone would assist in expansion, but I'd like to experience more abundance in an atmosphere uncluttered with fewer potentials for limitation. Yet, because I am aware of how 3D works and still not ready to fully trust, I fill out intrusive necessary forms and submit the fee to be investigated by the owner's condo association.

A month later another unexpected offer, much more abundant in possibilities, arrives. I gladly take it to share a lovely three-bedroom home, with much lighter energies, where I live alone for eight out of the twelve months rented.

✡

Human Interactions And Separation

For human mothers, especially those struggling to survive, it is heart breaking to see very capable adult offspring in turmoil. A Higher Self message comes though as I ponder supporting my beloved daughter until she gets back on her feet.

"I am a lost aspect of your soul waiting as many others for recognition. Call me what you will. The dis-ease within is a separation from Source. All of humanity feels this separation very strongly now. The current course of events is a necessary one to get all involved back to the wholeness of Self though recognizing their small self of one in another.

"The entire family is involved in this process and you, as the human mother, play your role best by maintaining the solidarity of Oneness for all gathering those aspects to merge back into the cohesive unity it was so long ago. Allow me to explain further...

"All that is happening now is the result of past efforts to separate from the Whole of *All That Is*, I know this does not seem to help in your 3D world but you must remember, you are not in essence a human. This separation is now ending and must first be recognized to do so. Do you see how each human interaction has served to bring the family together? This is the reason for the happening.

"This trial is on the verge of ending and you as the mother play a huge role. For it is you who have chosen to separate from the others in this lifetime. This separation is not of the essence of your soul but a lost aspect of soul searching for more experience. This experience is nearing it's end and all you need do is continue to follow the guidance within. That does mean to tap into the intuitive senses, check in daily, to determine the best course of action, or non-action.

"I leave you with this thought, as your world changes, the time to return to Oneness quickly approaches."

And now several years after my daughter's untimely transition I get more of the picture. As souls, we come to experience, life after life, each playing a different role and usually with the same group of souls. In the end of our playtime on earth, we must come into balance, to balance all those lives and incorporate all those parts of our self, recognizing we are One.

✡

I AM Ever With You

"I am ever with you. Do not be afraid as you move through this process of returning to full sovereignty. This process will continue for quite some time, for many on your earth. But keep faith for it is ever steady progress for those with full hearts.

"I am ever with you. Do not be afraid as you move through this process of becoming more alike with each day. Your process will be different from many as you do not strive but ease into new situations, new places of BEing, new awareness's of the One in which all live.

"I am ever with you. Do not be afraid as your earth continues to change at a rapid rate. Those ready to do so return to the Whole of *All That Is* as many others chose to play the game of becoming more in tune with her. I am ever with you. Do not be afraid as old things fall away to be replaced by new.

"I am the BEingness of *All That Is*, within each part of the Whole and I am ever ready to assist you."

This was a very different energy than what I have become accustomed to channeling. My heart beat faster and writing hand tingled, as if falling asleep as I wrote the words coming into my brain. When the message was complete, loose stools rushed me to the bathroom.

✡

Imagine Your World

"As you walk through this doorway of Love and Light, know we are with you. Your world continues to change as all realms watch from above. You are entering other galaxies of thought, other modes of living, other ways to be true to your Self. We share your joys as this period of earth time morphs further into the grandness and greatness of Self. Let all else fall away. Concentrate on the grandness of your True BEing and know we are with you all the way. Do not focus on those aspects of earth life you do not wish to experience but motor toward new experiences of abundance and Love. Imagine, my dear, imagine your perfect world and it shall manifest quickly as all else falls away.

"We are the White Winged Consciousness of Nine here to guide as desired all those ready to step forward into the Light of Oneness."

Finally, I now receive a practical step to take, "Imagine Your World."

As I go through my bedside notepad, transcribing more than a full month's messages on August 31, 2014, fighting with the extreme tiredness after eating breakfast, I again imagine my world. My world is full of like-minded friends, all ready and willing to share, bartering their gifts, talents, services and possessions for the good of humanity. My world is filled with abundance in health, joy, love, Truth and community. I live in a beautiful sanctuary by the sea and am happy to help others get the recognition for their work that they so richly deserve as I also receive the same recognition. Life is full of a balance between giving and receiving, between work and play, between family and friends. I continue to have all needs met before they arise and remain ever grateful to stay in the flow of good, the God Network that sustains and nourishes all life. I am very grateful to enjoy close relationships with several friends of like-mind as we join forces to help humanity. My car is always reliable, getting me to wherever I need to be safely and affordably. I truly am living a conscious life, aware of all thought, words and deeds, while helping humanity to recognize its spiritual magnificence!

✡

Journey Of Love

A message comes after a long restless night of runny nose, great thirst and many bathroom trips.

"And so it is my child. You have come far on your journey of Love. We, parts of you, parts of *All That Is*, have come to welcome and congratulate you as you reach these greater heights of awareness in your understanding of the world, the universe, the cosmos, the Truth of you.

"We are with you as you pave the way to greatness in form and formless states. We are with you as you move through the chaos of earth untouched. And we applaud your tenacity to continue on this great journey of knowing, 'Ye are Gods of Matter in physical form'. We leave the channel with one last request:

"Be aware of the greatness around you and applaud it as well. And so it is."

✡

Keepers Of The Flame Of Truth And Light

A different energy flows through me on the morning of 12/14/14.

"We are the teacher of the former Most High, the Keepers of the Flame of Truth and Light. You will work with us on a daily basis when the time comes. For now, you must rest your physical frame to be able to withstand the energies now upon earth. It is of the utmost importance that you take the time to listen in the wee hours of the morning. You shall do this by retiring early in the evening to assure enough sleep. Do you comprehend?"

"Yes," I answer.

"We will commence shortly. Be ready to write."

"What is your name?" I ask. "How shall I refer to you?"

"Seek above."

✡

Letting Go Of Control

Another much-welcomed message comes while learning that I must move again, amid ongoing family turmoil. It seems that each time I move more of the old life is left behind, both consciously and unconsciously, and I am nearly to the point where nothing remains of the old 'me'.

"You are that of which *It* is. There is no need to fear as you move though this process. Yes, you are becoming Light but it will not occur for you in this lifetime. Your task is to incorporate those aspects of yourself that were lost in the fray of forgetting. For you specifically, there is an issue with the blood that is corrected easily and efficiently by the love of self. This love of self has escaped you for aeons of time. Now is the time to indulge the senses in community and join with the forces of Light in your world in bodily form."

Feeling distraught, I ask, "What can I do?"

"You are coming to a point in your development where all things are known. This is a time of great change and challenge but you are up to the test (not that there is one). We are with you as you make the journey to further soul growth. Trust in the process and know the network that surrounds you will care for your needs as you become aware of the advice and follow the synchronicities. This is not a unique issue for you or many others, but it is an issue

206

many will face as this earth changes. We are with you all the way. You need only ask and we shall advise. We are the White Winged Consciousness of Nine here to assist."

✡

Lightbody Holding And Building

Massive coronal holes in the sun continue to affect many humans this entire month of April 2018. For me that means exhaustion, vaginal pressure at night, runny nose, watery eyes and rising every ninety minutes or so to urinate. My falling asleep time is now near one' o clock in the morning and I do not rise for the last time until nearly noon. At some point, a message comes so I turn on the bedside tape recorder.

"We are with you now as you move through these changes. The progress is steady and smooth for some and not so steady and smooth for others. The earth changes rapidly and along with these changes the human psyche, consciousness, changes as well. Knowing all is one, knowing all is, after all, illusion in your mind of one, the small one, it is still of the utmost importance to continue the practices of holding and building the lightbody. These practices are much more easily done when one is with ones self rather than in groups of uninformed people.

"Each human has chosen its path carefully as a soul and now is the time that many souls step away from their families, from the group consciousness in which they were raised and believed to be true, to move into their own state of increasing awareness of the Oneness of all life. This Oneness is not an illusion. This Oneness is of *All That Is* and ever will be and this Oneness does not change. As the human form takes on more of the attributes of the lightbody, it becomes necessary to achieve awareness of this Oneness.

"This Oneness will help all as moving through these changes progresses more smoothly and fluidly for those that know the Truth. Ye are gods in human form and that human form continues to change at a steady rate with these waves of consciousness entering the earth's atmosphere. This step towards Oneness is a necessary process to move though the body changes fluidly, progressing at a state unheard of on any level of awareness.

"Know that all are watched over carefully. Know that all, each form is guided. It is only in the small mind of one that chooses not to listen to the guidance received, not to believe the guidance received, that one continues to enter the field of mass chaos, which is now upon your earth. Know that all those who listen to the guidance within, all those who have honed their human body to the point where only Love and Light can enter, will continue to be guided through this process with smooth and steady progress. The Oneness of which you seek is already yours and we cannot stress enough to remain within that Oneness of the small self and within that awareness that ye are human gods in matter, now changing the course of humanity in an unheard of way.

"We are the Lemurian Council of Twelve and we are with you always."

It became a bit difficult to channel as I continued to lie in bed on the cusp of waking and disruptive construction noise began, so there may be more of this message to channel at a later time...

✡

Limitation Is In The Mind

As I wonder why I have not been approached with a housing offer or found a suitable, inexpensive place to move to, and as the application for re-certification for food stamps comes (yes, many lightworkers appear unsupported by those lost in the maze of forgetfulness), I ask for guidance as to why this is happening.

"The situation you are in is about playing the game, as you say, like a master, keeping in mind that the only limitation is in your own mind. This is a periodic course of events to help you hone your mastership. All you need do is play the game, keep the wolves (so to speak) at bay by giving them what they ask for (countless invasive forms to fill out), while recognizing your independence and abundance. It is a matter of not fighting the energies but moving along with the flow, pretending to play the game as everyone else and yet knowing you hold the keys to the abundance card.

"It is only a short time before this abundance will be clearly evident in your life but for the time being it is prudent to recognize this wholeness and abundance joyfully during each wakeful moment of the day and during sleep.

"We are the White Winged Consciousness of Nine here to assist as you ask but we cannot offer any more information to change your experience. You must use your own intuition and allow your Higher Self (as we are part of that Higher Self) to guide you in all ways."

It occurs to me several years later that our idea of limitation and abundance changes with our state of awareness. For those still lost in the maze, abundance may be owning a home, a car, house furnishings and other things. While others may believe, abundance is having an affordable roof over ones head, enough food to eat and the ability to do as one pleases without putting oneself or those things in jeopardy.

✡

Listen To The Voice Inside You

Technical difficulties begin as I work on the computer. It's a sure sign that there's a message to be heard while dusk gathers outside my beautiful two-story living space, which is a mere three houses from the beach of Fort Lauderdale, Florida.

"You must listen to the Voice inside you to feed your soul. Your world is changing at a rapid pace as many fall by the wayside, so to speak, with the inability to morph their mind and physicality to be more in tune with higher energies. There is a great change taking place upon your planet at this time and you must listen to the Voice inside you to carry you through tumultuous times.

"We are with you always, in light and dark, to shine your path with words of hope, truth and wisdom beyond your mind/body comprehension. It is with the greatest of respect that we ask you to take time daily to listen to the Voice within for, as time wears on this will become increasingly important.

"We are the White Winged Consciousness of Nine here to assist all those ready to remain on the path of ever-increasing evolution."

✡

Matching Thoughts And Emotions With Greater Awareness

"You are moving on to a higher state of awareness. We are the Keeper of One here to help you. It is with the greatest respect that we ask you to remain aware of your thought and emotions. Match these with your greater awareness at all times and watch your world change before your human eyes.

"It is your charge and the charge of many others to bring in this New Earth, this new way of living for all of humanity. We are the Keeper of One here to assist as asked. Remain open to receive the gifts that are rightfully yours.

"You will know when the time is ripe to move on for the conditions will be perfect for you to do so. Do not concentrate on conditions or timing in the present moment but remain thankful for everything and show that gratefulness in various ways. Show that gratefulness to each and every person in your life to open new doorways that will lead you to new beginnings.

"We are the Keeper Of One here to assist as needed and knowing you know, we are an aspect of you, an aspect of *All That Is*, Self, your Self with a clearly recognizable name. How may we assist you?"

It has been one of those days of mourning the loss of both my beloved children as a human mother and so I reply.

"You may assist me by continuing to remind me to put ego aside when conditions are not to my liking for often when not alone I feel stifled. I often wonder why I am not supported."

"Ah, but you are supported. Do you have an idea of where you would be if you were not?"

"Yes, I do and it would be in much worse conditions than this."

"And so continue to know you are supported. It is all experience and expression of the soul and it is all the experience your soul chose to have. We know that does not make it easier on the human host, but you must realize that unseen realms support you in this process seeing the experience and expression unfold in a way that is the least intrusive and disruptive to your human host.

"We are aware of the soul's choices. We are aware of the distractions the soul chose to overcome. We are aware of the many necessary roadblocks (to allow soul experience and expansion) that are currently being overcome and we caution you to remain in gratitude with a full heart. We caution you to be at ease in all situations even knowing you still are not there yet. We ask you to continue to trust in the unfolding Divine Plan. Pay attention to what is in your life and nourish it. Let go fully of what is not in your life."

And so I now live with more gratitude for what I do have knowing my soul (yes, illusion that it is as well!) is reaping the benefits of this human experience to expand, express, and contribute to the Whole in greater ways than ever before.

✡

Morphing Physicality

As dusk descends on this rainy Sunday, a communication waits to be documented while I enter the past two months of journal notes and messages. I finally set the spiral notepad aside to listen.

"These body changes occurring upon your planet are necessary to stay in alignment with Mother Earth. As these necessary changes take place, be aware that they are not geared toward any one group of human beings but include the whole of humanity. You must remain heart-centered to withstand these changes, in ever-increasing waves of change, for leaving your mind open to separation and fear only sets you up for defeat.

"The physical changes within humanity will continue for quite some time but be not dismayed over the process. Many are moving fully into this new body of Light, left so long ago to relish in denser energies. It is now time to return to your true BEingness and that is what is occurring today and everyday upon your earth.

"Your sun indeed plays a role in these changes but is not the only source of change. Body functions, DNA, tissues, cells, fluids and organs all morph as these changes continue. Your world also continues to change and may separate in areas not expected. Those of you leading humanity's morphing process shall know when these changes occur and will continue to be guided to safe land. There is no need for concern. All souls have chosen their journey in this and subsequent lives. Do not concentrate on the journeys of others but pay strict attention to your own journey. For you are the One of *All That Is*, each in it's own physicality, experiencing, expressing, and expanding as desired by each unique soul.

"We are the White Winged Consciousness of Nine ready, willing, and able to guide those moving forward with this morphing process, as desired."

✡

Moving Right Along

"It is important for you to remember, all things now move at a rapid pace upon your earth. You must relay each circumstance, situation, in your mind to move through old beliefs to get to newer, higher energy understandings. The things upon your earth will continue to change for years to come. But do not let this dissuade you as you go about your work. You and many others will continue to forge ahead, bearing the Light of One. The old ways of greed and manipulation will continue to be apparent in your world but you must continue to focus on the Light of your True BEing. That will never change.

"We are the Keeper of One ready to assist those willing to move forward."

As this message came through, it was hard to document, for my body, for the first time, rocked back and forth and in a counter-clockwise motion, as if to undo aeons of past beliefs. It continues to move even now as I rest after receiving the message.

✡

Moving Toward The Nirvana Of Heaven

Today, I move the first of my mere two closets of belongings to live in a stranger's spare bedroom, fifteen miles to the south, one block off of a major highway and less than two miles from Miami.

"You are quickly moving toward the nirvana of Heaven as you make the changes necessary to purge and cleanse old habits and ways of living. This process is necessary for you to move on to much better surroundings, experiences and people to assist on your journey. We leave you with this thought: as your world changes, remain in the positivity of the moment and know your world is the only world of your own making. We are the White Winged Consciousness of Nine here to assist as you seek a better life for yourself."

A few years later now in my own lovely second-floor apartment, I see clearly how the stay in a stranger's home, who is now a very good and loving friend, was in perfect Divine Order. It stopped me from being able to interfere with another soul's plans and helped to ready me for the experience I currently live.

✡

Physicality Expresses Itself Through Experience

This message comes on the Friday (two weeks before my sixty-fifth birthday) that my beloved 41-year-old daughter takes her own life in a second floor room of a small, quaint beach hotel (most likely hours before the event, but I am not aware of the loss until the next day).

"Physicality expresses itself through experience. Your expression of this experience is what makes the difference in your life situation. Each experience is molded with your thought based on your emotions. Pay careful attention to your thoughts and know they are molded with the emotion you feel throughout the day and night.

"We are with you to guide you but we cannot mold your emotions nor your thoughts. You must do this alone. Take care in the days ahead and know you can have the life you wish to live by molding thoughts with emotion.

"We are the White Winged Consciousness of Nine here to assist as asked."

✡

Radiating Light

This is the second day of heavy rainstorms in the area. Between downpours this morning, street construction continues for hours, very loud pounding of cement and horns, alerting people that huge trucks are backing up, constantly. I choose to move into my conscious living mode, going between sleeping to radiating Love and Light from the heart's core. This is an effective practice to use during stressful times such as living in the middle of heavy construction, discord or natural disasters. A short message comes on the cusp of waking near ten o'clock in the morning.

"You will move forward on your teaching path as you relate these conscious living tips to all who listen. Remember, it is your world; it is the world of those you see, you interact with. All living consciously can change this world and it is done one soul at a time.

"We are the White Winged Consciousness of Nine and we are here to assist."

✡

Rectifying Mis-Thought

Upon waking in the wee hours of this 64th birthday, I recall a dream in which my departed son Daniel hugged me. It was not the usual hug but arms reaching, as if from the heavens, to encase my body in a hearty, loving clasp. And then a message, which I quickly rise to document, comes.

"We come here to rectify mis-thought and deeds in previous incarnations, always with the intent of remaining within our own Self of One. But as we enter the atmosphere, all the intention is lost in the ethers of time and space. Humanity is now remembering those intentions as the strong energies of Christ Consciousness permeate earth in these last days of your year 2014.

"Awaken the Self within by remaining within your own thought system. Disregard those thoughts not in tune with Oneness and know you are part of a much bigger picture than you can possibly imagine.

"We are the White Winged Consciousness of Nine here to assist humanity through these momentous times."

Indeed, it is truly a momentous day. After we set up the classroom for the evening's Ascension Chair Ceremony, my friend Phillip performed some kind of odd ceremony to reconnect my silver cord. He boldly said, "You're not going to die now."

I hadn't told him that it is now the time of my planned demise, eight years after I stated the thought to my then husband, James. I've spent these past few years with no thought for tomorrow thinking I'd leave my physical body before turning 64-years-old. And today, I'm happy to still be here, recharged, compliments of Phillip, with a promise of even greater world service and abundance! What a birthday gift and he didn't even know it was my birthday today! I am so very grateful for this opportunity to serve humanity in new ways with more friends of like mind. Connections are being made each time we meet and it's clear, as the masters note, we have all been together in other lifetimes.

✡

Reluctant Lightworker Message:
Leaving Physicality

One should know, I am what many would refer to as a 'Reluctant Lightworker' very rarely asking for messages from unseen higher realms. The majority of messages that come through this host come on the cusp of waking or drifting off to other dimensions. Today after setting my small self aside as rain pours down from gray skies before the next full moon, solstice and 8/8/2018, I ask.

"Are there any higher realms that desire to relate a message to humanity?"

Of course, a message comes.

"We are the White Winged Consciousness of Nine and we wish all to know, all are loved and watched over very carefully despite the tumultuous activities upon your earth. As these New Earth energies continue to settle there are many things we shall relate in time. This is not to say that your time on the New Earth will always be filled with turmoil but to relate that despite what one may experience all is indeed in Divine Order. This is, after all, a soul choice to experience life in physicality, to experience what it is like to forget ones true roots, to experience what it is like to return to those true roots after many believe there is no such thing but turmoil, chaos and disruption.

"We are here as a group of souls long ago having experienced earth life to relate, all is not lost, for nothing is gained nor lost in your experience. This may seem ill advised to believe but we want all to know your experience is yours alone, based on aeons of thought forms and decisions left upon the old earth form from the beginning of your decision (as a soul) to experience physicality. We want all to know; as we did, you too shall return to the living and BEing experience in all aspects when your soul's experience has reached its end. That time has come and is coming for many souls now upon your earth. These souls chose to leave the earth experience to continue a journey of experience in other realms of existence before finally returning in all aspects to the Truth of BEing, which no form has ever left in True Reality. This may seem difficult to follow but know all on earth chose to experience physicality as souls. All on earth are now making the decision to leave this game, if you will, or return to the full knowingness that ye are not only gods of matter but so powerful that ye have experienced life in physicality without ever leaving the Whole of One.

"All on the New Earth now conclude their journey and return to the joy of BEing, of knowing the Truth has never left their essence of awareness. It is only in the small mind that one appears experiencing life in physical form.

"We leave you today with this thought:

"Is it your time to leave physicality? If so, perhaps you may wish to welcome the energies of Oneness and Love those within your current dream."

✡

Restructure

As the human drama in my personal life continues unabated, a welcomed message comes.

"Never fear. You are going through this process with your daughter to restructure thoughts, feelings and emotions. This process will take some time but it is your soul's choice, both your souls' choice, to experience. We of the higher realms are with you all the way even through it may feel as if you are alone in the process. We are carefully guiding you both as you move through this process and it is your soul's choice to do it in the manner in which you experience it.

"There are much more changes taking place on this and other realms that you will never be aware of. Trust in your soul's plan to move swiftly and smoothly as things in your world unfold at a greater pace now.

"We are the White Winged Consciousness of Nine here to assist. We may not be able to offer you human choices, for it is your soul's decision, but we can offer advice and guidance on a higher realms basis. We love you both. We are you."

✡

Returning To 3D

After studying *A Course In Miracles* and realizing that this world is not as I believed it to be, I gave up on seeking outside myself or seeking interactions with other people. This message came to me after a few years of acting like a hermit and less than eight months before my daughter successfully commits the act of suicide.

"There is much work to be done. It is time to move forward on the path to Oneness and Light. You shall accomplish this by returning to the 3D world left eons ago to be more in tune with the new energies to help those within the confines of separation. It is only from within that you are able to reach those aspects still not ready to merge with the greatness of Self. It is only from within that you shall become aware of the vast differences in being still experienced on your planet.

"We are the White Winged Consciousness of Nine here to assist as all move forward on this path of Oneness."

✡

Returning To 3D Intensifies

Shortly before renting a room from a complete stranger and a mere three months before my daughter chooses to leave this world of form another message wakes me.

"And so it has come to this, we must accept our humanhood, so to speak, to be as a human even while knowing we are indeed spirit in human form. The time is here to face the 3D reality of living as a human for you, my dear. This is but a short blip on the radar screen of your soul life, a time of great growth, great sorrow and great joy to begin.

"You have all you need inside the physical form to guide you. Ask for this guidance to receive it and know we, your unseen brothers and sisters of light, are with you always. This is a game you chose to play and master and this shall be accomplished in this life if you bear the Light of One fully and completely, barring no thought nor experience. We are the White Winged Consciousness of Nine here to assist, as always."

Yes, I spent several years alone, locked in my own dream world and knowing this world is not what it seems. And yet the time comes for us all to live with this knowledge while still seeming to be in the dream of forgetfulness. And because of our trials, our tribulations, our great sorrows and joys we are better able to help those seeming outside ourselves that are living in 3D, while we enjoy the beauty and abundance of 5D, incorporate and balance soul experience to end the game forever.

✡

Seeding The Planet With Nine Events

"The cosmos now enters intergalactic space to allow a more fluid receiving of planet earth. This receiving is meant to help all on earth coalesce with the greater realities of Oneness, of Truth and Light. This seeding now occurs as all on earth adjust to the new frequencies, new energies, brought about by waves of consciousness. These waves have entered your atmosphere compliments of your sun. The great central sun continues to spew forth these greater realities, for humanity must not tarry in the midst of darkness for it is time to awaken to the trueness of Self.

"All on earth are ready to accept this process or they would not be on earth at this time. This process is one of greater Love and Light for humanity has now passed the point of no return to darkness. The greater realties before planet earth now seed the planet with the Truth of original BEingness, but before planet earth reaches that point in its time/space continuum it must accept its extra-terrestrial original origins. *All of humanity is extra-terrestrial.* Nothing on your earth was there before what many refer to as the big bang. All life came from intergalactic space. Your cosmos is one of many moving through this process, but your particular cosmos is the only one that hosts the human form and therefore is of specific/particular attention to those unseen realms surrounding all space and time.

"These waves moving though and approaching your planet continue to create greater possibilities of awareness, of true BEingness. This is **one of the nine events**. The waves coming into the consciousness are one of these nine events. And as these events occur, humanity awakens on an even greater scale than ever before.

"The next great event now moves through the consciousness of humanity as these waves cement greater realities. The **second event** is more of a human nature, for it is a change in systems of government. These systems shall now include intergalactic communication, intergalactic awareness, and open partnering with intergalactic beings now widely known throughout your earth. This meaning the people of earth shall now become aware of the partnering of intergalactics within your government. This is the second event.

"The **third event** moves forth through the awakening of consciousness for humanity as well. This third event concerns the financial aspects of your planet. These financial aspects will now be more open and fluid for all humans, for no one being or one group will be able to secure financial success without other human beings afforded the same pleasure.

"We are aware of the channel's inability to smoothly coalesce these energies and we await the time when greater probabilities will help it to move though this process with more grace and ease. This probability/possibility is coalescing with these events.

"The **fourth event** upon your planet earth is one of more open Oneness among the people of planet earth. Each human will become more aware of its Oneness with others. Each human will become more aware that it is not on its own island of awareness but is also part of the humanity in which it finds itself. Each human will now seek to move within this sea of consciousness to help others, to help other humans within this Oneness of the New Reality of BEingness. The BEingness humanity moves toward is a BEingness without form, a BEingness that many entities now enjoy after having experienced form, in other places, in other spaces and times of your illusion, the channel's illusion, the illusion of all those who now read or hear this message.

"The **fifth event** for humanity is of catastrophic nature to earth. These necessary earth changes help to bring in these greater realities, the seeding of your earth. This seeding of your earth occurs through these so-called catastrophic events.

"The **sixth event** within the planet earth is one of a great awareness of ones own power as co-creator, the co-creator in earthy form, now changing.

"The **seventh event** within your earth is this change of physical form. This physical form now coalesces to be more in tune with that formless being, that ethereal formless being that inhabited planet earth in the beginning of time and space. This whole BEingness shall not take place for quite some time. It is not necessary to report this timeline for it will not occur in the timeline of any human that is now in form.

"We give you this **eighth event** now with great anticipation knowing that all are aware of the possibility, the return to the Lemurian aspects of humanity, no longer in form as it is now, but in the ethereal BEingness achieved upon proceeding this planet in the new space and time.

"The **ninth event** occurs after this eighth event of awareness of the ethereal form. It is the return to the BEingness for all Truths, all Light. Space and time disappears into the illusion of where it was created and henceforth, all return to the BEingness of Oneness, of Light, of Truth that it has never left.

"We are aware that the channel knows this information and yet has chosen to live within this illusion, within this awareness of consciousness and knows not of the illusion. We congratulate all of humanity who now graduates towards this awareness. And we are grateful knowing that more aspects of the True Reality of BEingness now know and live the Truth of Oneness.

"We are the White Winged Consciousness of Nine and we are here, as desired, to assist all to move though this illusion on earth of time and space."

Obviously, to me, these events are not listed in the order they seem to be occurring... We continue to experience the waves but sometimes I sleep better, waking only every ninety minutes or so to use the bathroom and trying not to drink water during the night. Yet, sips of water and sovereign silver are a must. And now after channeling this, my first eighteen-minute message upon waking for the fourth time after eight o'clock in the morning, I rise to eliminate before returning to bed to rest again.

✡

Soul's Charge

As I ponder establishing a website about building the Lightbody, the White Winged Consciousness of Nine flows through me.

"Again we wish to inform you it is your soul's chosen contract to help others with the process of returning to the Lightbody left so long ago. You were one of those who first relinquished this form and it is your soul's charge to be one who returns to this form to show the others it may be accomplished. This process may not occur in your lifetime but you will make great strides in helping others to return to this form. Do not be concerned with the process nor the time it takes for you are fulfilling the soul's contract and that is all that matters at this time.

"We are the White Winged Consciousness of Nine here to assist as you listen. Pay attention to the subtle energies and move through the flow of newer consciousness."

✡

Sovereign Powers

A message comes one day after the 2016 U.S. Presidential election.

"The world is changing quickly as all watch from ethereal realms. We are the White Winged Consciousness of Nine here to assist humanity as it moves through this evolutionary process of recognizing the True Self of each individual human. Each human is not aware of the sovereign power they hold but this power will now spurt forth as all call to their leaders for answers. Every step humanity takes on the scale of evolution makes a difference for other realms of consciousness as well. So it is with great interest that these other realms of Reality watch and offer assistance as it is desired by humanity.

"The power lies within each human and will now burst forth as these days move toward a crescendo of Hope, Light, Truth, Love and Prosperity for all on earth.

"We are the White Winged Consciousness of Nine and have more to relate as the channel through which we speak becomes more accustomed to these new higher realms energies that now assist her and humanity."

This message was difficult to write because fingers on the right hand became numb and tingled.

✡

Speak Your Truth

"It is time to speak your truth, Gatekeepers, Gridkeepers, your specific actions help to cement the crystalline grid. Your earth changes rapidly as all unseen realms watch from afar, distant galaxies, distant planets, and yet, distance is only a state of mind. It is time to speak the truth of the Law of One. In coming days, all shall become more aware of this Oneness as your world yet again experiences mass confusion, mass chaos. This is yet another new beginning for humanity and Mother Earth. The Law of One, simply stated, you are a part of one another; you are part of the Oneness of *All That Is*. You are part of the very consciousness that fills the air, between, within, among you. Go out and spread this word of One to all who seek it. It is time for the Law of One to be practiced once again. This is done by treating others as yourself, knowing you are each a part of the Oneness of all things."

In my mind, I ask for a source to name, even knowing it is all illusion and every message comes from my own consciousness. If I must name a source for this message, I hear, make it Amanda.

"I am Amanda and I come to you now as part of the entity through which this channel comes. It is after all only one."

✡

Stand Back: Chaos On Earth

Energies continue to be erratic as full moons, planetary alignments, eclipses, and coronal holes in the sun continue while humanity moves closer to 8/8/18, commonly known in some circles as the 'Lion's Gate'. In addition to canned foods, a stock of good quality water, toilet paper and Kleenex now sits in my closets as the hurricane season progresses. A message comes as lawn workers move through the community.

"Stand back as things unfold upon your earth. Those ready to move forward in their awareness of Oneness now stand back as the chaos of earth continues at an unprecedented level. This chaos is a necessary construct (idea) to help all recognize the Oneness in which all exist. This chaos brings together those still left in the mire of separation for it is only through chaos that one reaches out for another, seeks the assistance of others, opens with the compassion and love for others. Chaos brings forward those very aspects of consciousness, of Oneness. Chaos brings forward those very unlimited qualities of unconditional love, compassion, caring and truth upon your earth.

"This process unfolds now as your Lion's Gate opens on August 8th. This date is a date like many other dates and again, only those who have chosen to move though this portal shall do so. These portals are open at all times. Many move through them despite the dates on your calendar. As each soul's awareness

239

awakens within the physical frame the portals open and the physical frame changes to be more in tune with these portals as the physicality softens to a more ethereal form.

"As those of you who chose to do so move through these portals remember, there are other aspects of your own awareness still waiting for recognition. These aspects shall reach out to be recognized. One must always pay attention to what is in their unique energy field. Be aware of the subtle differences in energies within and around your own physical form and know that these differences are clues to allow you to coalesce more completely with the Oneness of which you truly are.

"We are the White Winged Consciousness of Nine and we here to help process those in this matrix of ill beliefs."

✡

Stemming The Flow Of Spirit

Some people know I am a rather reluctant wayshower due to past life experience and experience in this life as well. Today's message comes as no surprise as my departed daughter, Wendy, steps aside so the White Winged Consciousness of Nine can deliver a message that pertains to those of resonance (Wendy's messages to humanity are in *After Death, Communications...WOW!*).

"Reluctant lightworkers, wayshowers and starseeds have their reasons for stemming the flow of Spirit. Many have suffered tremendously in other lives being tortured for beliefs, others ostracized from family, friends and community at large in past and/or current lives and some even leery of speaking out due to fear of end results. Yet, the time has come for all world servers to set aside these experiences, these beliefs, some of which are from other lifetimes, to declare the truths they came to reveal.

"Humanity, lost in a sea of forgetfulness, forgot that all are One, unique in expression and form but nevertheless part of the Whole of *All That Is*. Lightworkers, wayshowers and starseeds it is time to step forth more fully to complete your mission. It is time to bring the Light of One to earth on a more consistent basis for it has never been needed as much as it is now this being the last Golden Age of 2,000 years.

"Many of you shall move on to other realms when your task is complete on this earth to serve in greater realms of responsibility. Some will return to earth in a new form to continue their service but make no mistake, your task is unique in itself and no one can complete that task as well as you can. It is the reason many other souls chose you to come to earth, to be the one that fits your shoes so perfectly.

"We are the White Winged Consciousness of Nine here to assist all of humanity and we especially wish to convey to all lightworkers, wayshowers and starseeds: you are not alone. You have never been alone and you shall never be alone. An assembly of guides is always nearby to surround and guide you. All you need do is ask for assistance. If you are not a clear host to hear us, there will be those in the physical realm who reach out to you or to whom you are guided to ask for assistance. But make no mistake; it is your god-given right to tap into your own Source Of Truth for guidance at any time."

✡

The Bottom Line

Intense energies continue to bombard those of us sensitive enough to feel them. A message comes after a long, restless night of repeatedly waking to recall experience after experience of different realities. I wake hearing, "The bottom line is" and know it is something to document.

"The bottom line is... nothing exists. Nothing exists in this universe or any other universe. Nothing exists in this reality or any other reality associated with time and space. Nothing is worth your fear, your worry, or your pain. Nothing is worth you giving up the True Self that you are. Nothing is worth allowing anyone or anything to change the unique aspects that you came to display as this earth game concludes.

"We are the White Winged Consciousness of Nine here to assist all humanity as the ethers mold more frequently to the Oneness of which It is"

This life filled with many opportunities to forget the True Self, in others and in myself. And it is only now, after seeming to lose two beautiful, pure children who did the same thing, to please others rather than themselves that I realize it is all about remembering who we truly are and why we are here.

We are here as spirit that took on a soul (which manifests different human vessels to experience different aspects of human life) to learn unconditional love for others and for ourselves. We are here to learn; we are unique aspects of the very thing many of us pray to. We are aspects of Consciousness, God, whatever you choose to name it, here to help others and ourselves awaken from the illusion of separation.

Yes, it is time to **WAKE UP!**

✡

Transition Of The Ages

"We are the White Winged Consciousness of Nine and we are here to assist humanity in this transition of the ages. Your world continues to undergo radical change as all upon her continue to wake up to their spiritual magnificence by losing the things they hold dear or by making changes in their perception through other avenues. We are here to guide you, as always, as these changes occur. Call upon us, as you desire, whenever you wish to tap into the Source of all things, the Divine Spark within you.

"For you, my dear, we are here to insure that your mission is met with the utmost grace and ease. We are aware of your many planned distractions and will continue to guide you if you wish. Yet, you need only focus on your heart to make all decisions, using the mind as a guide. You would not give everything away and be homeless as a rule, but know that what you need (for survival) is necessary to live in the world in which you have agreed to participate in.

"This is a clear state of being, of matter, and you are finding that your fears can no longer lead your actions. Continue to meet your fears head-on and you shall see there is nothing to fear."

This message came two months after my daughter's transition. All I can say is that after the transition of both my children, giving up most of my possessions, divorcing my husband

and living in places I never sought to live, looking at life from a soul point of view makes it easier to continue life and think with my heart. AND send the straightjackets; my bottom line is it is all illusion anyway.

✡

Travel In Both Worlds

The bedroom light turns on by itself so I listen for the message that is sure to come.

"The best choice is to travel with one foot in both worlds. Count on the abundance that you are but also take steps to insure it, guided by synchronicity. Allow things to come to you, without pushing your energy onto others. Seek only the pristine awareness of the One within."

✡

Trust Your Soul Plan

Once again, I ask my Higher Self to interact with me, to announce when the best time is to move, etc.

"Your resonance and discernment awaits fine tuning while you wait to move into your perfect sanctuary. Yes, indeed, it is time to move away from the ego-oriented way of living and trust more fully in your Higher Self to guide you. This is a new situation for many on earth at this time and I, your Higher Self, ask you to be more patient with your own ego.

"It is understandable that the ego wishes it's own place in which to live without another's presence nor interference but this, as you are now becoming aware of is not your soul's plan. Your soul now has plans underway to move into community more fully and yes, you will be interacting with many more people in your world, online, on phone, via internet, but especially in person. This is a necessary course of events as your world changes for humanity and for your soul's plan. The mission of your soul is a hearty one this time around, as if you didn't know,

"It is in the best interest of your physical self to stay where there is as less interference with the vibrational rate as possible while these mass changes occur. This is done in a place not of your own (not one where I am listed as the occupant and with a lease and utilities to pay) but one in which others are thought to dwell. Yes, you shall remain where you are until September. Your compatriot will leave and you shall find your perfect place in September but until that time, I ask you to be patient, to have faith in the process that is unfolding.

"Yes, I am aware that you doubt the occurrence of this, as many dates have been mentioned but this is not only as you would note a done deal but one that meets most fully with your own soul plan. I ask that you trust in this process. Yes, you can move before the time in September but the dwelling to which you move will not be as spectacular as the one to which you would move in September. That is all you need know."

On 1 September, I do move into a rented one room, private cottage with full kitchen, bathroom and two yards, blocks away from my first Florida residence.

✡

Unseen Assistance

"You are blessed with the richness of *All That Is* to finish your task here on earth. It is with the greatest pleasure that we assist you, and others, from higher realms of existence. All lies in readiness to move forward in the Christ Consciousness that you all so lovingly seek. It is but a short time span away. But in the meantime, there will be some heavy burdens to carry for those not yet ready to return to the Wholeness of One. There are many of you to help these lost souls and it is our great pleasure to assist you.

"We are the White Winged Consciousness of Nine here to announce that the energies and powers you seek already lie within you."

My body now rocks back and forth, as I read this dawn message before returning to sleep. Extreme thirst, with bouts of water intake and elimination accompanied me for the past two nights. Bloating, extreme thirst and vivid dreams ruled tonight.

✡

Ways To Move Out Of Limitation And System Greed

"Your world changes quickly as your government moves forward with its efforts to stifle the people. This is not something to be ignored but a heads-up on world affairs. There is a great global change taking place on your planet and you would do well to continue your own work alerting the people of what is to come. This is not your role to be a doomsayer but you can do this through your departed daughter Wendy. You can alert those that need to hear the truth of their BEing. You can do this to help them discover ways to move out of limitation and system greed.

"We are the White Winged Consciousness of Nine here to help as desired. Thank you for playing your role despite your circumstances."

And so *After Death, Communications... WOW!*, the book, begins.

✡

What You Think Becomes Reality

"You are beginning a new process whereby all that you think becomes reality much faster than before. You are one of many on this earth to make great changes and it is with these changes that humanity shall awaken from its deep sleep of forgetting the true matter of One. It is in these next few days especially that the time of humanity moves to a new timeline for many, again. It is in these next few months that humanity again changes into an unrecognizable state for many people.

"Do not allow this to dissuade you from the task at hand, to spread the Light of One on this earth knowing all are One and shall never be separate. We are the White Winged Consciousness of Nine here to assist as desired but we cannot assist without your agreement and efforts to listen. Do you understand?"

"Yes," I answer.

"We shall commence our messages with you now that your right and perfect place has arrived."

I moved months later. The woman who owned the one-room efficiency cottage continued to go though trials and tribulations pulling me into them. And the place was not as perfect as I'd first thought but I most certainly fulfilled my soul's contract with her.

✡

Wild Ride

So many questions but gut feelings must lead the way...

"This is the way for you to connect more fully with your soul plan. You chose this experience for yes, you know what is coming and it is best to be with those of your soul family to ride this storm together. We are here to tell you the ride will indeed be wild but this is something you have chosen to experience for soul growth of all involved. You are an intricate part of this plan to experience, express and expand.

"We leave you now with this blessing. Your plights will be few; your treasures will be many. Although bumps will be along the road, we will guide you all the away. Do not fear we are ever near.

"We are the White Winged Consciousness of Nine ready to assist as asked."

✡

Winds Of Change

Hurricane Irma's winds have finally knocked out the neighborhood's power so I now turn the laptop on to transfer more channels onto the computer (well prepared with two fully charged laptop batteries). But before I begin, and the core reaches us in an expected two-plus hours, I take the time to ask...

"Is there anything I need do now?"

"We are with you now as these winds of time shift and change the very nature of your world and neighborhoods. We are keeping close watch on those ready to report and listen. It is time to report the trends of the New Earth and this will be done by those moving through these vast changes. You all came for this final call and it is with the greatest of pleasure that we watch while you bravely weather the trials and tribulations on your earth.

"For you personally, you have taken the necessary steps and all is in readiness for your next phase. Continue to listen to that still, small voice within to guide you in the hours ahead. It is all we have to relate at this time. You are safe in your neighborhood hammock, nestled in a place that is secure from stronger destructive winds and rain."

Although both trees in the backyard uprooted and one fell onto the roof of the bedroom (where I slept knowing of the possibility but allowing myself to move with the flow) there was no damage to the house itself. Power remained off for ten days but I was well prepared. Friends helped to keep me cool by bringing ice, which I promptly placed on body areas as needed to cool down between cold showers. They also periodically recharged my portable power system, allowing me to recharge cell phones and use small appliances.

✡

~ Part Three ~

Affirmations

Returning To The Purity Of
Oneness, Expressing Our True Self
Fully, Helps To Free Us From The
Limitations Of Earth.

"I AM ever so grateful for the **fearless peace** that moves within and surrounds me."

♥

"I now consciously agree to **accept all offers and gifts**."

♥

"I AM Perfection unfolding on earth in **Prosperous, Healthy, Joyful and Loving Form**."

♥

"I am ever grateful to be conscious of, and to use, the tools necessary to keep this body in **physical perfection**."

♥

"I AM that of which *It* is, **perfect, whole, complete, and abundant** in all things good, always **having whatever I need** before the need arises and for this I am ever grateful!"

♥

"I bring down the **wisdom of higher realms** to guide me in all thoughts, words, and actions in this reality."

♥

"With ease and Grace, I **nurture the Light of humanity** through good thoughts, words, and deeds."

♥

"I bring down the **abundance of Higher Realms** to experience in this reality and am ever so grateful to do so."

♥

"I AM a **powerful creator with the ability to manifest a New World**. I now go forth and use my powers to manifest this world now."

♥

"I am ever so grateful to **reflect the wisdom of my Higher Self**. And I bring that wisdom to all realities."

♥

"I bring down and incorporate the **wisdom of Higher Realms** to use in this reality."

♥

"I AM a master at **manifesting** all things good and I manifest them now **through my thoughts, my words and my deeds**. I AM and so It is."

♥

"I am ever grateful to bring more of the **fifth dimension into this reality** as I go about my day."

♥

"I am grateful for the Light in me that continues to sustain this **body's perfection.**"

♥

"I now with Grace and Ease **clear all that is not in the best interest of my soul plan.** I now with Grace and Ease fully **accept my sovereignty** and move forward to the New Earth **free of all limitation.**"

♥

"I hereby **release all bands of consciousness that block the Higher Self.** I am **open and receptive to wisdoms from higher realms** and I am ever so grateful to receive them."

♥

~ Part Four ~

Conscious Living

Be conscious throughout your day!

A Glimpse Into Light

WOW! I was in bed, on the cusp of waking, moving in and out of dimensions (I consistently ask to remember being in dimensions where I am more conscious than I seem to be in this one). My friend and I seemed to be at Poverello thrift store, but we were there for work, scanning the shelves of sale items to look for materials that we needed.

One of the things my friend and I were looking for was napkins. As I looked at the shelves of napkins, a number of beautiful, ivory-colored linen napkins caught my eye (several years ago, I gave away such beautiful, nearly brand-new napkins). I thought they were nice and perhaps I should take one home with me. Then I thought, no, I do not need to take one. One napkin was marked $5 in black permanent marker and I thought that stupid, thinking the napkin was ruined and no one would purchase it with the price marked on it. Upon closer inspection, I saw that the $5 price was marked onto a wide piece of tape that was taped (I taped something before bedtime) to the napkin so the linen was not destroyed. So then, I thought I'd take one of the napkins because it would look nice in my place. Then I forgot what I was doing and asked myself, "Wait a minute, what was I doing?"

My friend now seemed gone and I tried to get back to the napkins but all of the sudden I seemed to be sucked out of the room, backwards. The scenery kept changing as my body kept moving and I couldn't control it. I was sucked out of scenes and kept moving, flowing faster and faster. Continuing to watch scenery, I moved faster and faster, and at one point began to panic.

"Wait a minute," I said. What's going on here? What's happening?" I asked.

And then I told myself, "Just go, just go with the flow."

Now I seemed to be in forward motion, just watching the scenery without emotion and moving towards something, no longer backward but able to see what I approached. I was still being pulled forward but now there was a brilliant, golden-yellow wall of Light way ahead of me. The wall was **not** well defined but seemed to morph into the scenery from which I was coming from. It was a very fluid coming together of golden-yellow Light and scenery. It appeared that once you reached the Light there were degrees of Light, deeper and deeper shades of Light to move into.

I continued to flow towards the Light. But before I reached the Light a noise within the dimension where my body lay in bed caught my attention. It was the movement of bedroom vinyl window blinds. My mental body then had to determine how that noise woke me because the windows were closed and, I thought, there was nothing to rustle the blinds. But then upon opening my eyes, I realized that a cloth laid at the bottom of the blinds (to block out a gap of harsh lighting from outside during the night). The cloth had fallen off causing the blinds to waver and wake me with the noise.

Of course, right away I grabbed the tape recorder to document this grand experience! Hopefully, next time there will not be anything to pull me out of that dimension and I shall complete the experience. It was wild! It was a good, wild experience!

Pay attention to your dreams for they often consist of multiple dimensions in which you can play. Before sleep, tell yourself you will remember your multidimensional travels and bring down wisdoms into this New Earth. The return to Light is now in steady progress!

I should note that while we do mind travel into other dimensions while sleeping there is also a lot of brain processing from this dimensional life going on. There's more about dreams in my book *Bits of Wisdom.*

Changing Habits To Return To One

Humanity continues to move through energies increasing consciousness, what Steve Rother and the Group refer to as waves (twenty-two for 2018). There are seven waves in April alone. Energies are very strong and many people sleep much more and have other signs of a changing body. Sleep is inescapable for me as I am in bed for ten to twelve hours during the night, nap an hour or two after eating the first meal near noon, but still wake every 90-minutes or so during the night to void water. I am now reaching those other dimensions of a greater reality and last night experienced another doozy of a dimension...

So, if this is a dream world of our own making and we continue to return out of habit, obviously the way out is to change habits. The habit changed within the dimension of this sleep time was of disbelief of the power to move through what appears as solid objects. In this dimension, the location seemed to be Tibet for the houses were lighter, gold colored with beautiful gold trim and fascia. I saw a moving train and a moving house. The train was on the tracks and looked as the houses but slimmer and moving on the tracks. The house was much wider and taller and moved along with the train but on the ground. At one point, they both seemed to adjust easily down into the ground, but not all the way; they kept their fluid movement forward but more of the train and house seemed underground. And then they moved back up making the train and house more visible above ground.

At one point, I seemed to be moving with the house and as the house moved it began to shift though what seemed solid gold-colored walls. As we approached the first one, I reminded myself to go with the flow and was guided to just close my eyes and not react. The key to moving though the walls was to know you could and not hold any fear nor denial of the ability to do so. I moved though several walls along with the house and each one seemed a bit denser and darker. I then woke up in my bed for what I think was the seventh time, to rise for the day at 11:30 a.m.

Enlarging The Consciousness Of Oneness

Of course, since it will be one year tomorrow, and I am working on our book of channels, my daughter Wendy comes in unexpectedly after a busy day of soup making and sharing.

My departed son, daughter and I are now balanced souls, meaning our joint life experiences are balanced. I have incorporated them into my own soul essence to begin the process of Oneness. And I recognize that I have now consciously done the same thing with each other family member who left physical form.

It is now my charge (Wendy did not say this but I now recognize it) to consciously incorporate the essence of each soul that now passes from physicality. I came to carry this signature (along with other positive signatures such as prosperity) into my last (next) incarnation. This is how humanity will reap the Oneness we so desperately need, by recognizing each soul as part of *All That Is*, by incorporating each soul's essence into our own, enveloping it, enlarging the consciousness of Oneness within each of our unique physical minds to carry into our soul's energy field and eventually be One again in all aspects. It is an honor to know I was chosen among many souls for this blessing!

Helpful Tips & Tools

- Be aware of the wounds and defenses of other people.

- Believe in your powers of manifestation. Write down your wishes, your dreams, and your hopes. Put them in written form to view throughout the day and view them with great knowledge that they are already yours.

- Pay attention to thoughts, words and deeds. If they continually dwell in separation, that is what will appear.

- Focus on positive ways to spend time. Read inspiring books, attend and participate in groups that focus on Oneness (*A Course In Miracles* and *A Course Of Love* are two such groups).

- Spend time alone without the distraction of electronics and news. Become accustomed to listening for higher realm guidance rather than counting on mainstream media or others.

Merging Back To One Body

As you continue to merge all bodies, bring down the aspects of each into this and all subsequent and known realities. The following are some affirmations to repeat before bedtime.

"I now bring forth greater states of awareness and BEing to this and all subsequent and known realities and am ever so grateful to do so."

"I now bring down and incorporate wisdom to this and all subsequent and known realities."

"I now bring down the highest form of abundance to this and all subsequent and known realities."

"I now bring greater possibilities for humanity, from higher states of awareness, into this and all known and subsequent realities."

Moving Through the Portals

Many of us are grounding New Earth energies. In addition to the usual signs (mainly body aches and pains, digestive issues, dizziness, extreme exhaustion, abrupt changes in body temperatures, high pitched ear ringing, hot soles of the feet, memory loss, sinus issues and sleeping disorders - - due to transmuting parallel lives), we also abide by many other rules and habits. These include the disregard for usual ways of living. We no longer feed old energies of greed by shopping in retail stores. We no longer spend large sums of money for overpriced entertainment or unnecessary goods and services. We dedicate our lives to helping others in need and take all circumstances in our lives as signs of where we are along the path of ascension. So consider these ways of living if you are experiencing grounding signs and know your own resonance and discernment is the best guide to lead you through portals.

Neutralizing Chaotic Energies: Radiate Love

As energy waves of consciousness continue to enter earth, people are affected in different ways. Some people deal with this energy by being angry. We can help those and others around us by spreading Love and Light if we are ever in the midst of anger. For instance, in the community where I live sometimes people are very angry, yelling when energies are high. When this occurs (and other times such as during heavy construction), I radiate Love from my heart's core to fill the area. This not only helps the body of which my soul experiences physicality, but helps the community as well for remember everything is energy, radiating out into space. So, when you focus on your heart's core and radiate that loving energy out into the world, you help not only your body but the bodies of all those around you. And that radiation of loving energy continues to spread throughout the earth and beyond it. This is a very practical tip that one can use during times when it seems the anger within people is increasing. Remember, the result of chaos is nirvana but we must first move through the chaos. You can choose to match and feed chaotic energies or you can choose to neutralize them and nurture harmonious thoughts by radiating loving energy out into the world.

Opportunities

In the likely event that you are wondering, "What is going on in this world???"

YES, things are changing rapidly. Humanity is quickly, or not, changing into the state of mind it left so long ago.

For some, that means being faced with circumstance after circumstance of separation, in our own mind, until we realize WE ARE ONE. We are NOT separate. Each person we face is, indeed, a part of our very own self. Yes, the small self here on earth seems separate but we are now faced with the BIGGER picture of *Reality*, WE ARE ONE in seeming, separate unique form here to experience life in bodily form on earth.

So what can we do if continually faced with situations that appear negative? We can see these situations for what they are, opportunities to recognize aspects of our self, to accept them with unconditional love and to let them go (if need be) knowing WE ARE ONE, WE ARE LIGHT, WE ARE part of *All That Is* here to shine and share our gifts with humanity.

Running Light...Not For The Weak Of Heart Nor Body

Running light through the physical mind/body system is not for those not yet ready to care for his or her self. Each energetic boost takes one to a whole new level of lightness, of frequency, if you will. With each burst of the sun, with each movement of planetary consciousness, with each move of earthy realms coalescing with the higher realms, we are building lighter, higher frequency bodies. This is not for the weak of heart or body. And those unable to withstand the now constant onslaught of higher realms energies will leave the planet en masse. They will leave the planet though a variety of means, body dysfunctions, medical mishaps, suicide, natural disasters and terrorist attacks. All those with a weak body and mind will leave as these energies continue to bombard the planet.

It is essential to care for oneself. Drink plenty of good quality water (if you can get it); eat lighter foods and meals; abstain from tobacco, excessive alcohol consumption; and negative energies. Keep your living space free of clutter and disarray and know the higher realms are here to assist all those ready to move forward with this new earth game (never before played on any planet, time or realm of space).

Know the one you seek lies within you and is now coming forth to lead the way to freedom from the self-imposed enslavement humanity brought on itself by taking on denser and denser forms.

The time is now. Be ready to make the change or in coming years leave the planet to play on other realms until ready to return to Oneness in all aspects.

Seven Keys To Live By

1. Stay open to possibilities.

2. Move into new situations with an open mind.

3. Feel into your heart using your heart to think instead of your mind.

4. Use your internal gyro-system; resonate with your heart (then) think with your mind.

5. Know you are never alone and are guided every moment of every day and night.

6. Stay within your own wisdom and mode of thinking. Do not adhere to another's rules of life unless they resonate with you; use your heart and gyro system.

7. Remain aware that each person you interact with is your mirror. Pay attention to their messages.

Wobbling Realities

Energies continue to be exhausting and various body maladies occur out of nowhere. Just days ago, I had difficulty walking because a large vein popped out of the back of the right knee and was very painful. Yet, knowing the body continues to clear, cleanse and transmute energies of a lower nature, it just seemed best to rest and care for the body instead of seeking outside help. And of course, as many times before, the condition improved greatly in two days and is now gone.

As usual, sleep has been erratic but much better than previous years. Vivid experiences of being on other dimensions of reality – dreams where there seems no greater consciousness of mind than this current state – seem to rule two-hour periods of deep sleep. Today, after asking to bring down something from a higher state of awareness this knowledge came...

On the cusp of waking, you feel the wobble (I feel it consistently now) of realities in which you can tap into. Sense each one to decide if it is one you wish to enter. For instance, you may wish to enter a wobble (dimension) to rectify mis-thought or change a negative experience or bring down wisdoms from greater states of awareness. To do this:

1. Feel the wobble cluing you into different dimensional realities.

2. Sense each one, asking if it is a reality you wish to enter to either:

Clear, cleanse and transmute outdated concepts.

Bring down wisdoms into the current reality.

Play and have fun.

3. When you determine the wobbling reality you wish to enter, merely agree to enter and mindfully move into the wobble.

For some souls with many lives, this is a good way to clear thought forms. And for those who have come to teach it is yet another way to bring down wisdoms from past lives.

Definitions

Below are selected definitions within the state of separation from *All That Is*.

Aeon ~ Also, known as eon; an age or immeasurably long period of geologic time, usually longer than an era. Aeons/Eons are divided into eras, which are in turn are divided into periods, epochs and ages. The time of recognizable humans – the three million year Quaternary period – is vastly small compared to previous aeons such as the Hadean (before fossil record of life on Earth), the Archean, the Proterozoic and the Phanerozoic.

Awakening ~ Awakening from the dream of separation, also known as spiritual awakening. As unique expressions of *All That Is* we decided to forget our true nature to play a game called earth life, for the purpose of experiencing and expressing in physicality. (Refer to the Preface in *Book Of One :-) Volume One* Lightworker's Log.)

BEingness ~ The true state for those figments of *All That Is* that chose to play the game of separation. It includes your physicality on earth, your soul in other realms and your Essence in *All That Is*.

Dimensions ~ Bands of Consciousness (yet another imagined separation from the true VOID of all BEing) in which separated (in mind) aspects of *All That Is* experience, express and expand their consciousness. 3D is where humanity resides; 4D is where consciousness abides during sleep and human death; 5D is conceived as a 'higher' playground where higher realms exist such as ascended masters and angels. Humanity is now moving into the New Earth (5D reality where everything known from all lives and states of human consciousness is dissolved allowing the return to Oneness and subsequently the VOID, as desired by unique states of seemingly separate Consciousness).

Earth's New Breed ~ Humans with more of the original DNA blueprint who do not carry the usual human unconscious guilt. They choose (as souls) to be born in physicality as highly intuitive and sovereign beings for the purpose of humanity's evolution.

Golden Light Downloads ~ Frequencies of Light (waves of Consciousness) that are always apparent and usually experienced more readily during full moons and planetary alignments. These downloads help humanity adapt to the New Earth.

Higher Self ~ May also be referred to as Self with a capital S. See Self of One.

Host Of One ~ Humans/Souls choosing to play the game of separation by sharing the concept of Oneness.

Law of One ~ An Eternal Truth of **non**-separation operating on all levels, with connections among everything. As humans, we have placed many thought form layers between ourselves and the void from which our essence came and it is now time to diminish and release those thought forms to end the game of duality and separation to live as One again in all aspects.

Light of One ~ An ethereal form of experience containing all of those unique essences, aspects of *All That Is*, desiring to experience life in other richness of BEing

Mind of One ~ A state of awareness that is a perfect state of BEing, devoid of separation.

One ~ The truth of our BEing, one Truth, one Light, one Life in which all unique aspects of the Whole of *All That Is* reside.

Self of One ~ May also be referred to as Higher Self. A higher state of human consciousness where one is tapped into their own heart-based guidance system and closer to the truth of One.

Small mind of one ~ The small mind of one is the egotic mind consisting of thought forms of the current personality.

Soul ~ A temporary tool created by a unique essence/spirit to experience, express and expand its consciousness in physicality by taking on various human forms.

Souls Of One ~ A conglomeration of all souls chosen to be in earth form for the purpose of extending the knowledge of Oneness throughout humanity and the Cosmos.

Sovereignty ~ To be totally independent - within your own truth - and to know that you are supported by unseen guides.

White Winged Consciousness of Nine ~ A group of souls who lived as humans. They now help humanity to self-empower itself to sovereignty and to free all souls from reincarnation.

Wounds and Defenses ~ Behavior that protects egotic ways of living. Defenses are unconscious reactions that protect wounds. An example would be acting superior as a defense to hide the wound of feeling inferior.

Prologue

Humanity is now in the process of gathering dispersed light from previous forms (human and non-human). When the process is complete, humanity shall return to the original form of LIGHT! Yes, it makes sense that humans dispersed LIGHT out of previous forms due to the density of its nature! The more forms taken on, the less LIGHT within subsequent forms. Fortunately, the tiny Divine Spark within each human heart remains, as a rule, to allow this gathering of LIGHT.

About The Author

SAM, author of the "Lightworker's Log Book Series," is a minister (ordained by Sanctuary of the Beloved Church Priesthood and Order of Melchizedek), channel of higher realms, metaphysical teacher, founder of SAM I AM PROductions (**SamIAMproductions.com**) and administrator of the popular Internet resource, Lightworker's Log (**LightworkersLog.com**). Spreading Spirit's message of Oneness throughout the globe, SAM is a wayshower helping others to learn the truth of BEing so humanity can return unique figments back to *All That Is.*

The Lightworker's Log Book Series

Book One: Death of the Sun

Book Two: A Change in Perception

Lightworker's Log :-) Transformation

Manifesting: Lightworker's Log

Prayer Treatments: Lightworker's Log

Adventures in Greece and Turkey

Earth Angels

Return to Light: John of God Helps

Bits of Wisdom

Book of One :-) Volume 1

Book of One :-) Volume 2

Book of One :-) Volume 3

Book of One :-) Volume 4

After Death, Communications...WOW!

www.ingramcontent.com/pod-product-compliance
Lightning Source LLC
LaVergne TN
LVHW051456080426
835509LV00017B/1781